—TH
FOOD
COOKER

THE FOOD AID COOKERY BOOK

EDITED BY
DELIA SMITH

FOREWORD BY
TERRY WOGAN

BRITISH BROADCASTING CORPORATION

'Go, eat the fat, drink the sweet wine,
and send a portion to the man who has nothing . . .'
Nehemiah 8

For Africa with love

Published by the British Broadcasting Corporation
35 Marylebone High Street, London W1M 4AA

First published 1986
Reprinted 1986 (twice)

ISBN 0 563 20492 3

Typeset in 10/12 Garamond ITC by PFB Art and Type Ltd, Leeds
Printed in England by Chorley and Pickersgill Ltd, Leeds
and Redwood Web Offset, Trowbridge, Wiltshire

CONTENTS

PREFACE

I suppose the seeds of FOOD AID were planted with *that* pop record at Christmas 1984. Somehow the words struck a deep chord in me. I had no idea at the time what would happen, but come that sunny July day in 1985 when I watched the world rejoicing with such unity and purpose, it seemed to me we were witnessing a celebration of life: warm sunshine, music, joy and all of this would in itself become life-giving.

Well, it couldn't end there, could it? Especially as the results were so phenomenal, £65 million in just a year. If pop singers could give the gifts they have, what about cooks, what about the food industry? What Bob Geldof has proved is that giving and sharing need not be a solemn guilt-ridden affair.

It seems to me that whilst we need to do all we can to fight and eliminate famine by sharing at every level, we also have a responsibility to rejoice in our own good fortune and *appreciate* the good food we have. The FOOD AID Cookbook is, I believe, a combination of both – every recipe lovingly given and lovingly cooked and enjoyed will at the same time be continuing to help relieve famine in Africa.

I would like to thank Bob Geldof for his inspiration, and Terry Wogan and Frances Whitaker for mobilising ordinary cooks all over the country to send us their cherished recipes by the thousand. Thank you, all senders, for your generosity. I'm so sorry we couldn't include the whole lot!

A thank you too to the FOOD AID team and to the publishers who produced this book in little more than two months, and finally a thank you to *you* for buying it. If you like it please buy at least nine more copies – that's approximately one a month till Christmas!

God bless

Delia Smith
Easter 1986

When FOOD AID was first mooted, as another source of funds for the relief of famine, it caused the odd lifted eyebrow, and doubt clouded many a finely-chiselled brow. Doubtless, the inspired and inspiring Geldof himself ran into whole brick walls of doubting Thomases while trying to get *Live Aid* and, before that, *Band Aid* off the ground, but thanks to the extraordinary Bob, aid for famine relief was now perceived by Those Who Must Be Obeyed as a *Good Thing* and one, furthermore, *To Which The Public Respond* . . .

Still, FOOD AID had its doubters. Was a recipe book full to bursting with exotic ingredients and expensive comestibles the right way to be raising money to help the starving? I put the point civilly to the present Mrs. Wogan. 'Well', said the gentle saint who has to put up with me and my children, 'I'm contributing a caviar pie to this gustatory extravaganza' (I don't know where she learned to talk like that) 'which sounds a pretty expensive way to stoke up the inner man, but if it helps to sell this book, why not? Just so long as it doesn't provoke a national outbreak of galloping indigestion . . . And anyway, I'm sure Bob Geldof didn't pause to consider whether anybody in the starving Third World had ever heard of Paul McCartney, David Bowie, Mick Jagger or himself before he put *Live Aid* together.' As always, the sainted woman was right. The *only* point is: that those of us who *can* afford good food ought never to lose sight of the unfortunates who can't even afford a handful of rice . . .

So dive in, without a Grecian bend, into the varicose viands, fine vittles, pies and puddens which you will find carefully detailed between these pages. I'm delighted that WOGAN played its part in gathering the myriad recipes from all over the country, from the great and the good to the average viewer in the kitchen. They've all been lovingly and skilfully collated by no better woman than Delia Smith.

Enjoy! Enjoy! And thank you.

Terry Wogan

SOUPS AND STARTERS

Princess of Wales' Watercress Soup

Serves 3

Recipe sent by HRH the Princess of Wales

The FOOD AID team are thrilled to be able to include a recipe from the Princess of Wales. Her attendance at the LIVE AID concert was what prompted us to ask her and now – as then – her own concern for famine in Africa has been a great inspiration to all involved in this book.

1 oz (25 g) butter
1 oz (25 g) flour
1 pint (570 ml) warmed chicken stock
2 bunches (about 6 oz or 175 g) fresh watercress
½ pint (275 ml) single cream
Salt and freshly-milled black pepper

Melt the butter in a saucepan, then add the flour and cook for a couple of minutes on a low heat, stirring gently. Now slowly add the warmed chicken stock until you have a creamy consistency.

Wash the watercress thoroughly and add it to the mixture. Cook slowly until the stalks are soft, stirring occasionally – this will take about 20 minutes. Remove the pan from the heat and allow the soup to cool. Liquidise the mixture in a blender or food processor, then pass it all through a fine sieve into a bowl. Add the cream (reserving a little to garnish the top of each portion), then cover the bowl and chill until ready to serve.

A few leaves of watercress, previously blanched, can provide additional garnish if required.

Sweet Red Pepper and Tomato Soup

Serves 4 people

Recipe sent by
Mandy Ashworth
Maidenhead
Berkshire

This is a very easy soup to make, but it has a really lovely flavour. We like it served with garlic croûtons (see page 189).

2 red peppers (approx. 6 oz or 175 g each)
2 teaspoons olive oil
1 medium onion (finely chopped)
12 oz (350 g) ripe tomatoes (skinned and chopped)
1 clove of garlic (crushed)
½ level teaspoon thyme (fresh or dried)
½ level teaspoon ground cinnamon
1½ pints (850 ml) hot chicken stock
1 tablespoon tomato purée
1 teaspoon lemon juice
1 egg yolk
Salt and freshly-milled black pepper

To garnish
Soured cream
Freshly snipped chives

Begin by pre-heating the grill to its highest setting, then place the whole peppers under the grill and, using a pair of tongs, keep turning them until the skin has become blackened all over. Then remove them carefully (they are very hot!) and leave them on one side to cool.

Heat the oil in a large saucepan and cook the onions until softened but not browned, then add the tomatoes, garlic. thyme and cinnamon and cook for about 10 minutes.

After that rinse the peppers under cold running water, and peel the skins off, cut off the stalks and remove the seeds. Now you can either chop them very finely by hand or chop them in a blender or food processor, then add them to the pan along with the stock, tomato purée and lemon juice. Bring it all up to simmering point and simmer gently for 10 minutes.

Allow the soup to cool for a few minutes before blending it to a smooth purée in a liquidiser or processor, then return to the pan and gently reheat to simmering point. Now take it off the heat, whisk the egg yolk first on its own and then into the soup. Return the pan to the heat and continue to whisk for about 2 minutes without letting it come to the boil. Taste and season as required, then serve with a swirl of soured cream in the centre of each bowl, sprinkled with chopped chives.

Kashmiri Tomato Soup

Recipe sent by
Gary Booth
Bath
Avon

Serves 4 people

This is a lovely and very different tomato soup, fragrant with the flavour of cardamum. We like it served with a spoonful of yoghurt swirled into each bowl and we love Gary Booth's idea of buttering the soup bowls!

1 lb (450 g) fresh tomatoes (skinned and chopped)
2 ½ pints (1.5 litres) cold water
1 large onion (finely chopped)
1 tablespoon ghee or oil
1 tablespoon wholewheat flour
1 tablespoon tomato purée
10 green cardamoms (crushed with a pestle and mortar)
1 inch piece of whole cinnamon
1 teaspoon salt
Freshly-milled black pepper

First of all simmer the tomatoes in the water for 10 minutes, breaking them up with a wooden spoon.

While this is happening fry the onion in the ghee or oil until it has softened, about 5 minutes, then add the onion to the tomatoes. Now mix the wholewheat flour to a paste with a little of the liquid, and then add this to the tomatoes. Next add all the remaining ingredients and simmer uncovered for 15 minutes. Adjust the seasoning to taste.

Next, strain the mixture through a sieve, forcing it through with the back of a spoon. Then reheat it, pour into buttered bowls and serve.

Note from Gary Booth: save the residue in the sieve, remove the cardamom pods and cinnamon and use the rest as a base for spicy rissoles!

Kashmiri Tomato Soup; Avocado Sorbet page 19; Mushroom Pâté page 20.

Thick Vegetable Soup with Melted Cheese Croûtons

Recipe sent by
Mrs A Humphreys
Thorpe Bay
Essex

Serves 6 people

This is a comforting soup to serve on a chilly, windy day.

2 large carrots (pared and coarsely grated)
2 large parsnips (pared and coarsely grated)
2 large onions (skinned and chopped)
1 oz (25 g) pearl barley
1 oz (25 g) red split lentils
14 oz (400 g) can Italian tomatoes (sieved)
1 level teaspoon dried mixed herbs
2½ pints (1.5 litres) vegetable stock (see page 187)
Salt and freshly-milled black pepper

For the garnish
6 slices French bread
2 oz (50 g) strong, matured Cheddar cheese (grated)

All you do is place the carrots, parsnips, onions, barley, lentils and tomatoes in a large flameproof casserole, sprinkle in the herbs, season with salt and freshly-milled black pepper and pour in the stock and bring everything up to simmering point. Then put a lid on, keep the heat very low and simmer the soup for about 2 hours.

About 5 minutes before serving pre-heat the grill to its highest setting. Sprinkle the cheese over the slices of French bread and lay them on the surface of the soup. Now place the casserole under the hot grill until the cheese has melted and become bubbly and tinged with brown.

Carrot and Caraway Soup

Recipe sent by
Michael Muir
Edinburgh
Scotland

Serves 10 people

Michael Muir obviously loves cooking and people. He likes to serve this soup garnished with heart-shaped fried croûtons of bread with the ends dipped first in milk then in parsley. He says this soup is a delicious combination of sweet carrots and caraway and is wonderful on a cold day after a rugby match!

2 lb (900 g) carrots
4 oz (110 g) butter

8 oz (225 g) onions (chopped)
¼ pint (150 ml) dry sherry
½ teaspoon salt
Freshly-milled black pepper
2 pints (1.15 litres) stock
2 teaspoons of caraway seeds

For the garnish
Croûtons
Raw grated carrot
Cream

First, cut the carrots into even-sized pieces, then melt the butter in a saucepan, then add the onions and caraway seeds and sauté these very slowly until the onions are golden (about 15 minutes). Then add the sherry, followed by the carrots and the seasoning.

Next, prepare a double sheet of greaseproof paper, large enough to fit over the vegetables in the saucepan, dampen with a little cold water then fit it close over the vegetables. Now put a lid on the pan and with the heat at the lowest possible setting, let the carrots sweat gently in their own juice and the sherry for 1 hour.

Add the stock and then liquidise the soup or blend it to a purée. Then pass it through a sieve. To serve, re-heat gently and pour it into warmed soup bowls and garnish each with a swirl of cream, grated fresh carrot and some croûtons.

Cream of Celery and Celeriac Soup

Serves 4 – 6 people

Recipe sent by
Mrs S Cleugh
London W10

This is a beautiful and simply made soup with a wonderful flavour – but it needs to be eaten on the day it's made as the celeriac tends to discolour with keeping.

1 lb (450 g) celery, chopped (reserve the leaves for a garnish)
1 lb (450 g) celeriac, peeled and chopped (weighed after peeling)
1 large onion (peeled and chopped)
2 pints (1.25 litres) chicken or vegetable stock
½ pint (275 ml) single cream
Salt and freshly-milled black pepper
2 oz (50 g) butter

First of all melt the butter gently in a large heavy saucepan and add the celery, celeriac and onion to it. Stir well to get all the vegetables coated in butter and keep the heat as low as possible. Cover the saucepan with a lid and sweat the vegetables, taking care not to burn them, for 10 minutes.

Now add the stock, salt and freshly-milled black pepper and bring everything up to simmering point and simmer gently (covered) for 40 minutes, or until the vegetables are tender. Then cool it a little and liquidise the soup, adjusting the seasoning. Then return it to the saucepan, add the cream and reheat gently before serving. Serve garnished with the chopped celery leaves and accompanied by some crisp French bread.

Pumpkin Soup

Serves 4 people

Recipe sent by Geoffrey Lawrance Bromley Kent

Pumpkin makes a very creamy, velvety-textured soup with a subtle flavour. Don't worry if the pumpkin flesh looks fibrous and old, it will be transformed in the cooking.

1½ lb (700 g) pumpkin
1 oz (25 g) butter
1 medium onion (finely chopped)
1 level teaspoon Madras curry powder
1 oz (25 g) flour
1 pint (570 ml) chicken stock
1 rounded dessertspoon tomato purée
½ pint (275 ml) milk
Salt and freshly-milled black pepper
1 sprig of parsley (chopped)

Peel the pumpkin, discard the seeds and surrounding fibres and dice the flesh into small cubes. Then melt the butter in a large (5 pint or 3 litre) saucepan, add the chopped onion and cook this over a low heat until the onion is soft, about 10 minutes.

Now raise the heat to medium, stir in the curry powder and cook for another minute. After that stir in the flour and cook for a further minute. Then stir in the stock a little at a time, followed by the tomato purée and the diced pumpkin. Bring everything to the boil, stirring continuously, then lower the heat and simmer very gently, stirring occasionally, until the pumpkin is soft (this can be anything from 15 to 40 minutes).

Finally, sieve or liquidise the mixture and return to the saucepan, add the milk and reheat gently, seasoning with salt and freshly-milled black pepper. If the soup is too thick you can add a little more milk. Garnish with chopped parsley.

Stilton and Leek Soup

Recipe sent by Miss H Griffin Tunbridge Wells Kent

Serves 4 people

This soup is simplicity itself and yet it has an unusual delicate flavour and tastes quite special.

½ lb (225 g) leeks (weighed after trimming)
2 oz (50 g) butter
1 medium onion (chopped)
1 pint (570 ml) vegetable stock (see page 187)
¼ pint (150 ml) milk
2 oz (50 g) Stilton cheese
Salt and freshly-milled black pepper

The best way to prepare leeks is to split them almost in half lengthways and then fan them out under a cold running tap to wash away any hidden grit. Slice them across into 1 inch (2.5 cm) pieces.

Melt the butter in a large, thick-based saucepan, add the leeks and onion, then cover the saucepan and, over the lowest heat possible, let the vegetables gently sweat in their own juices for 10 minutes. Stir them two or three times during the 10 minutes. Add the stock and milk, bring everything to a gentle simmer and simmer gently for 10 minutes, this time without a lid.

Remove the pan from the heat and allow the mixture to cool. When it has cooled pour it into a processor or liquidiser and add the Stilton, crumbled roughly. Blend the soup until smooth. To serve, reheat gently and check the seasoning. We think this is nice garnished with some very finely chopped spring onion and some cheese croûtons (see page 190).

Libyan Soup (Shouraba)

Serves 6 people

Recipe sent by
Mary El-Rayes
Hemel Hempstead
Hertfordshire

This is a stunning soup and completely different to anything we've tasted before. In fact, one of the delightful things about working on this book has been discovering such unusual recipes from all round the world. This would be an excellent choice for a dinner party served with warm pitta bread.

8 oz (225 g) finely chopped onion
2 cloves garlic (crushed)
2 tablespoons olive oil
4 – 6 oz (110 g – 175 g) finely chopped raw lean lamb or beef (not minced)
4 oz (110 g) chick peas (soaked for 12 hours)
2 oz (50 g) spaghetti (broken into short lengths)
1 heaped teaspoon ground allspice
1 heaped teaspoon ground cumin
1 heaped teaspoon ground coriander
2 – 3 heaped teaspoons mild chilli powder
5 oz (150 g) double concentrate tomato paste
½ – 1 fresh green chilli (de-seeded and finely chopped)
2 pints (1.25 litres) water
2 teaspoons sugar
1 teaspoon salt
2 tablespoons chopped parsley
1 tablespoon dried mint

To serve
Pitta bread
Lemon wedges

First of all heat the oil, then add the onion and garlic and cook until they are lightly browned, about 6 minutes. After that turn up the heat and add the finely chopped meat. Cook, stirring frequently, until the pieces of meat are all lightly browned.

Now turn the heat down and stir in the ground spices and cook for 1 minute or so before adding the tomato concentrate and fresh chilli. Then mix everything well and as soon as the base of the pan begins to brown add the water, then the sugar, salt and drained chick peas. Now put a lid on and simmer very gently for 45 minutes. After that remove the lid and sprinkle in the spaghetti pieces, re-cover and cook for a further 15 minutes stirring from time to time.

Lastly, stir in the parsley and the mint and serve with lemon wedges to squeeze into the soup.

Avocado Sorbet

Serves 4 – 6 people

Recipe sent by
Elizabeth Brooke
Lytham St Annes
Lancashire

This would be the perfect start to a meal that includes a very rich main course, especially if the weather is on the warm side.

3 large or 4 small avocados (about 1 lb or 450 g of flesh)
½ lb (225 g) peeled cucumber
3 tablespoons fresh lime juice (or lemon if not available)
3 level tablespoons caster sugar

To serve
Radicchio or lettuce and fresh mint

Halve the avocados and remove the stone, then quarter them and peel the quarters. Roughly chop the flesh and put it into a food processor or liquidiser, and use a teaspoon to scrape off all the very green part next to the skin and add this, as it does wonders for the colour.

Roughly chop the cucumber and add this to the avocado, then add the lime juice and sugar. Now simply purée the mixture until it is absolutely smooth and lump-free. Pour it into a shallow polythene container and freeze for a couple of hours. Then mash it with a fork to break it down and smooth it out before it solidifies. Freeze it again until it is solid.

To serve, remove it from the freezer and defrost for about 2 hours at the bottom of the fridge. Fork it again to break the sorbet down to make it malleable. Arrange some radicchio or lettuce leaves in the base of four (or six) wine glasses, spoon the sorbet on top and garnish with a sprig of fresh mint. To add to its aesthetic qualities, you could chill the glasses before serving.

Avocado and Pink Grapefruit Salad

Recipe sent anonymously

Serves 4 people as a starter

This, if you use pink-fleshed grapefruit, has a very attractive colour and the textures and flavours are lovely.

2 ripe avocados
2 pink-fleshed grapefruit
8 oz (225 g) potatoes

For the dressing
2 tablespoons olive oil
1 tablespoon lemon juice
½ teaspoon strong English mustard powder
Few drops soy sauce
Few drops Worcestershire sauce
1 clove garlic (crushed)
½ tablespoon mayonnaise
Salt and freshly-milled black pepper

Boil the potatoes in their skins in salted water, then drain and peel when they are cool enough to handle (if you are using new potatoes leave the skins on). Cut the potatoes into ½ inch (1 cm) dice.

Peel and stone the avocados and chop the flesh, then remove the pith from the grapefruit segments. These can then be cut into halves.

Now make the dressing by combining all the ingredients together in a screw top jar; shake it to amalgamate them. Now toss the grapefruit, avocado and potato in the dressing to get everything nicely coated and set aside, covered in a cool place, for about 3 hours to allow the flavours to develop before serving.

Mushroom Pâté

Recipe sent by Shelagh Noden Aberdeen

Serves 4–6 people

Shelagh says that 'this is a cheap and delicious alternative to meat pâtés' and we agree. It is excellent as a first course with hot fingers of sesame toast or for a lunch or picnic dish with crusty French bread or rolls.

8 oz (225 g) mushrooms (wiped and sliced) – the dark open kind are best for this
2 oz (50 g) butter
1 oz (25 g) breadcrumbs
2 level teaspoons finely grated onion
3 oz (75 g) softened butter
4 oz (110 g) curd cheese
A little freshly grated nutmeg
1 teaspoon lemon juice
Salt and freshly-milled black pepper

For the sesame toast
4 – 6 slices from a wholemeal loaf (crusts removed)
Butter
1 teaspoon sesame seeds per slice

To garnish
Fresh sprigs of watercress

First of all, melt the 2 oz (50 g) butter in a saucepan and add the mushrooms. Stir them all around to get a good coating of butter and then over a very gentle heat let them cook slowly till softened and reduced – about 15 minutes. After that stir in the breadcrumbs and allow to cool.

Add the mixture to a blender or food processor along with the onion, softened butter, cheese, nutmeg, lemon juice, salt and freshly-milled black pepper. Blend evenly and then remove it to a terrine or gratin dish (about ¾ pint capacity) lined with clingfilm or foil. Cover with clingfilm or foil and place in freezer compartment for 1 hour to set. To unmould, wrap a hot damp cloth around the dish to loosen the pâté. Repeat if necessary, then invert onto a serving dish and garnish with watercress.

To make the sesame toast, pop the bread under a pre-heated grill and toast each slice on one side only. Butter the untoasted sides completely, then sprinkle the sesame seeds equally and evenly over the buttered sides, pressing them down to keep them in place. Return the bread to the grill to toast the sesame covered sides until the seeds (and the bread) are lightly toasted. Then cut each slice into 4 fingers and serve with the pâté.

EGGS AND CHEESE

Cold Poached Eggs with Watercress Mayonnaise

Serves 3 people as a main course or 6 as a starter

Recipe by Delia Smith

This is my own offering to the FOOD AID collection. I have chosen it partly because it's so quick and easy, and partly because it's such an attractive colour. It is a variation of the egg mayonnaise theme, but a little bit different and even more delicious!

6 large fresh eggs

For the mayonnaise
4 oz (110 g) watercress (dried in kitchen paper)
2 large eggs
1 teaspoon salt
1 clove of garlic (crushed)
1 rounded teaspoon mustard powder
½ pint (275 ml) groundnut oil
2 teaspoons wine vinegar
1 teaspoon lemon juice
Freshly-milled black pepper

To garnish
Thinly sliced crisp lettuce leaves

Begin by poaching the eggs: fill a frying-pan with water to a depth of approximately 1½ inches (4 cm), then heat it to a temperature just sufficient to keep the water at a bare simmer. Then break the eggs (two at a time) into the simmering water, and let them cook for 3 minutes or so. As soon as they're cooked to your liking, use a draining spoon to lift them from the water and transfer them to a bowl of cold water. Then cook the remaining eggs, and leave them in the cold water while you prepare the mayonnaise.

Separate off the watercress leaves and discard the stalks. Now break the two eggs into the goblet of a blender or food processor, add the salt, garlic, mustard powder and a few twists of freshly-milled black pepper, then switch on to blend these together.

Next pour the oil in a *thin* trickle through the hole in the top with the machine still switched on. When all the oil is in, add the vinegar, lemon juice and watercress leaves, then blend again until the sauce takes on a lovely speckled green colour.

To serve, arrange thinly sliced lettuce round the edges of your serving plates to form a border, then arrange one or two eggs in the centre and spoon the dressing over and around them. Serve with crusty wholemeal bread.

Class 5's French Toast

Makes 6 squares

Recipe sent by Class 5 Worcester Junior School Enfield Middlesex

I was thrilled and delighted to receive a batch of recipes from all the children of Class 5 at Worcester Junior School, Enfield, Middlesex – average age 9 years. Many of them were beautifully written, some of them illustrated in colour with helpful drawings and others giving lists of equipment needed. I was very impressed by their kindness and effort. Two of the children sent us the same recipe – which one called 'Eggy Dip' and the other 'my best food', and which I call 'French toast'.

So here is the recipe beloved by Americans who serve it with cinnamon, sugar or maple syrup, or as a savoury with crisp fried bacon. Sam Ayriss and Nicola Gymer in Class 5 like it just as it is!

1 large egg
2 tablespoons milk
3 medium thick slices of bread from a small loaf (preferably a day old)
1½ tablespoons oil or 1½ oz (40 g) butter or margarine

Beat the egg together with the milk in a bowl (if you are going to serve it sweet with honey or maple syrup you could add a drop of vanilla essence here or alternatively a seasoning of salt and pepper if your preference is for something savoury).

Cut the crusts off the bread and cut each slice in half. Now heat the butter or oil over a medium heat. Then dip the squares of bread into the egg mixture, making sure they are well coated, and fry them in two or three batches for 1 minute on each side or until crusted brown. Drain well on absorbent kitchen paper before serving.

Mariner's Eggs

Serves 3 people

Recipe sent by Bista Giorgini Florence

These are the invention of a long-distance sailor (hence the name), and show what a little ingenuity can achieve with the most basic of ingredients, such as you might find in the ship's galley.

1 lb (450 g) ripe tomatoes (skinned and chopped) or a 14 oz (400 g) tin of chopped Italian tomatoes
1 large onion (chopped)
6 tablespoons (approx.) oil
½ teaspoon dried basil
1 teaspoon tomato purée
6 eggs
3 oz (75 g) freshly grated Parmesan cheese
3 tablespoons plain flour
Salt and freshly-milled black pepper

Heat 2 tablespoons of the oil in a medium-sized saucepan then add the chopped onion and cook to soften (but not brown) for 5 minutes before adding the tomatoes and basil. Then cover the pan and cook over a fairly gentle heat for 30 minutes. If the sauce still looks a little watery at this stage, continue to cook it with the lid off until it has reduced a bit, then stir in the tomato purée and a seasoning of salt and pepper, and keep the sauce warm while you attend to the eggs.

Pre-heat the grill and have a serving dish warming. Now heat 2 further tablespoons of oil in a frying-pan and separate the eggs, placing the whites in a mixing bowl and reserving the yolks in a cup (keeping them whole). Whisk up the egg whites until they are stiff but not dry, then combine the Parmesan and the flour with a little seasoning, and fold this mixture into the egg whites (don't worry if they deflate at this point, just keep working with a minimum of folding strokes).

Now drop tablespoons of this batter mixture into the hot oil in the frying-pan – to get six fritters in all. When golden-brown on the underside, flip them over to cook on the other side. Then arrange the fritters on the warmed serving dish, spoon a little of the tomato sauce over each one, make a slight indentation in the sauce with a spoon and slip an egg yolk on top of each fritter. Grill briefly to set the egg yolks a little, and serve straightaway with some crusty bread.

Note: It may be necessary to fry the fritters in two batches, in which case you'll have to top up the frying-pan with a little more oil.

Canadian Bacon and Egg Brunch

Serves 6 – 8 people

Recipe sent by
Phyllis Morrison
Co. Durham

Although using ten eggs sounds a little like Mrs Beeton, this is nevertheless a very quick and easy way to serve brunch to 6 hungry people. For fewer people you can halve the recipe, and for more (say 8) you can add some crisp sautéed potatoes. It looks beautifully golden and puffy – like a soufflé.

½ lb (225 g) thinly sliced Canadian bacon (if this is not available, thinly sliced lean back bacon with rinds removed will do)
4 oz (110 g) Swiss cheese thinly sliced (Gruyère or Emmental)
10 large eggs
1 tablespoon milk
Salt and freshly-milled black pepper
¼ pint (150 ml) soured cream

Pre-heat the oven to gas mark 6, 400°F (200°C). You'll also need a baking dish or casserole 8 inches in diameter and 2 inches deep (20 × 5 cm).

Start this off by lining the baking dish or casserole with overlapping slices of bacon, arranging them all over the base and sides. Then arrange the slices of cheese over the bacon.

Now take a large mixing bowl and whisk the eggs in it together with the milk, freshly-milled pepper and a little salt (be careful with that because of the bacon). Now pour the egg mixture all over the cheese and bacon, then spoon blobs of soured cream all over the top. Transfer the dish to the pre-heated oven and cook for 25 – 30 minutes until puffy but firmly set.

Helen Wogan's Caviar Pie

Serves 8 – 10 people

Recipe sent by Helen Wogan

Helen Wogan recommends this is served with smoked salmon (Irish of course) and Irish soda bread. We have an excellent recipe for the latter on page 128.

6 hard-boiled eggs (shelled)
2 oz (50 g) butter
Salt and freshly-milled black pepper
2 tablespoons finely chopped spring onions (or chives)
3 × 2 oz (50 g) jars of lumpfish caviar
2 × 5 fl. oz (150 ml) cartons soured cream

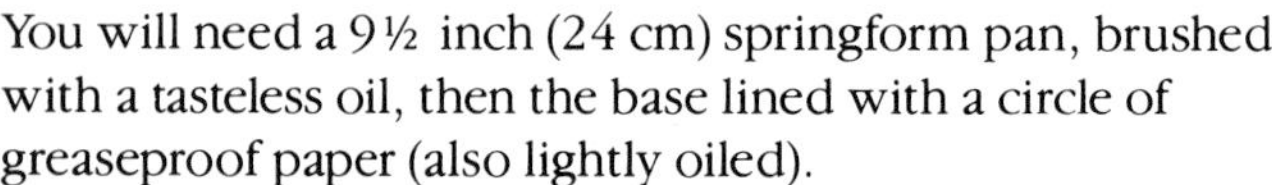

You will need a 9½ inch (24 cm) springform pan, brushed with a tasteless oil, then the base lined with a circle of greaseproof paper (also lightly oiled).

Put the shelled eggs, butter and some freshly-milled black pepper into a blender or processor and blend until smooth (it doesn't matter if the eggs are still a little warm). Taste and season well, then spread this mixture in the base of the springform pan, cover and chill for about 3 hours.

About half an hour before serving, spread the lumpfish caviar evenly over the eggs and sprinkle with a tablespoon of spring onions (or chives). Now spread the soured cream in a broad band around the edge, leaving a centre circle showing the black lumpfish caviar underneath. Sprinkle with the remaining spring onion or chives and chill until ready to serve. Remove the springform side but don't attempt to remove the base. Transfer to a serving dish and serve cut into wedges.

Börek (Turkish Cheese Pastry)

Makes 12 squares

Recipe sent by Ann Günal Amersham Bucks

Because Turkish cheese is not available we have adapted this to incorporate a mild English cheese, such as Lancashire or Cheshire and we like this best eaten cold with a salad but it would make ideal picnic food.

1 lb (450 g) puff pastry (can be frozen)
8 oz (225 g) white cheese (grated)
1 egg (beaten)
2 tablespoons fresh chopped parsley
Salt and freshly-milled black pepper
1 beaten egg (to glaze)

Pre-heat oven to gas mark 6, 400 °F (200 °C).
You will need 1 greased baking tin approx. 12 by 9 inches (30 by 23 cm), 1½ inches (4 cm) deep.

First of all make the filling by mixing the grated cheese, egg and parsley in a bowl; season well with salt and freshly-milled black pepper.

Now divide the pastry into 3 portions, then roll out the first portion to an oblong, 1 inch (2.5 cm) larger than the baking tin, and use this to line the tin, allowing the pastry to come up the sides. Now spread half the cheese mixture all over this and then roll out the second piece of pastry to fit the tin exactly and then fit this over the filling. Then spread the rest of the filling over that.

The last piece of pastry needs to be about ½ inch (1 cm) larger than the tin. Fit this over the last lot of filling and then dampen the edges with a little of the beaten egg (for glazing) and pinch it together with the edge of the first layer of pastry to seal it all round. If you have any uneven bits you can trim them with a sharp knife.

Now brush with beaten egg and bake in the centre of the oven for 40–45 minutes until puffed up and golden brown. Cut into 12 squares. You can serve it hot but it is nicer cold.

Cheese and Mushroom Strudel with Poppy Seeds

Serves 4–6 people

Recipe sent by
Julie Phillips &
Joanne Haines
Penzance
Cornwall

This is not recommended for the nervous novice cook as you need courage to get the pastry as thin as it needs to be. But for anyone who enjoys a challenge this really is a delicious hot supper dish; serve it with a fresh tomato sauce and a crisp green salad with a sharp lemon dressing.

For the pastry
5 oz (150 g) plain flour
A pinch of salt
1 egg
Approx. 1 tablespoon vegetable oil
Approx. 3 tablespoons lukewarm water
Milk
Poppy seeds

For the filling
3 oz (75 g) brown rice
4 oz (110 g) grated Cheddar cheese
3 oz (75 g) toasted brown breadcrumbs
1 medium onion (finely chopped)
4 oz (110 g) mushrooms (sliced or chopped)
4 fl. oz (110 ml) milk
2 oz (50 g) butter or margarine (melted)
Salt and freshly-milled black pepper

Pre-heat oven to gas mark 4, 350°F (180°C).

Make the filling up in advance by cooking the brown rice and mixing it with the cheese, breadcrumbs, chopped onion and mushrooms. Pour the milk over it, followed by the melted butter and season it with salt and freshly-milled black pepper. Cover and leave aside.

For the pastry, sift the flour and a pinch of salt into a mixing bowl, and then make a well in the centre and beat in the egg, the oil and enough water to mix it to a smooth dough (add a couple of tablespoons of water first, then add the rest only if you need to). The dough should be smooth and you should now knead it until it becomes very elastic in texture. This will take about 5 minutes and you'll need a little more flour to dust it with to prevent it sticking.

Now to roll it out you will need a clean cloth, approx. 1 yard (1 metre) square (a piece of an old worn out sheet will do nicely). Needless to say you'll also need some space to roll it out on. What you do is flour the cloth all over, and then pop the pastry on to it and start rolling and stretching the dough. Don't worry if you don't get a perfect square and won't worry if you get a few holes, they won't matter, but what *does* matter is that the pastry must be paper thin – will power is important! The pastry will eventually roll out to an area that almost fills the cloth.

Now you sprinkle the filling all over. It will look a bit sparse but that's OK, as next the whole thing gets rolled up. To do this, first fold each edge in about 1 inch (2.5 cm) and then lift one end of the cloth and just allow the whole thing to roll over and over like a swiss roll, tilting the cloth as it rolls.

You then need a large greased baking sheet – transfer the strudel on to it and fold it round into a horseshoe shape. Now brush with milk and sprinkle poppy seeds all over, and bake the strudel in the oven for 40 minutes. Serve cut into slices.

Cheese and Sesame Shortbreads

Recipe sent by
Joan Brady
Evington
Leicester

Makes 30 – 35

These melt-in-the-mouth little shortbreads are lovely, served as a lunchtime snack with soup.

4 oz (110 g) plain flour
2 oz (50 g) grated Cheddar cheese (must be a strong Cheddar)
2 oz (50 g) ground rice
3 ½ oz (85 g) butter (at room temperature)
¼ teaspoon salt
A good pinch of cayenne pepper
¼ teaspoon paprika
1 tablespoon sesame seeds

Pre-heat oven to gas mark 6, 400 °F (200 °C).
You will need 2 ungreased baking sheets.

First sift the flour into a bowl, then add the cheese, ground rice, salt, cayenne and paprika. Mix everything well, then add the butter and rub it in using your fingertips and finally bring the mixture together and lightly knead it into a dough.

Next, on a lightly floured surface, roll the dough out to an oblong, approx. 11 by 4 inches (28 by 10 cm), using the rolling-pin to knock back the edges to keep them straight. Next, sprinkle the sesame seeds lightly and evenly all over the oblong and roll them gently into the dough – they must still be visible. Cut the oblong across into strips, about ¼ inch (1 cm) wide, then using a fish slice or something similar, lift them on to the baking sheets and bake for 30 minutes. Cool them on a rack and store in an airtight tin.

Pashka

Serves 4 – 6 people

Recipe sent by
Nina Sagovsky
Claygate
Surrey

This is a traditional Russian Easter delicacy – it can be eaten as a dessert, cut into thick slices and served with crisp biscuits, or spread on a cake or sponge biscuits. Nina Sagovsky says that all families in Russia in the old regime had their own version and this one belongs to her family. It's traditionally moulded in special wooden moulds but Nina suggests a 5½ inch (14 cm) flower pot – which we found worked well.

1¼ lb (550 g) curd cheese (room temperature)
6 oz (175 g) unsalted butter (room temperature)
4 hard-boiled yolks of egg
1 whole raw egg
3 tablespoons soured cream
3 oz (75 g) crystallised pineapple (chopped)
1 oz (25 g) finely chopped blanched almonds
½ teaspoon pure vanilla essence
1½ oz (40 g) caster sugar

You will also need a 5½ inch (14 cm) diameter (top measurement) earthenware flower pot, scrubbed and sterilised in boiling water, and some muslin.

First place the curd cheese, unsalted butter, hard-boiled egg yolks and the whole raw egg together with 3 tablespoons of soured cream into a food processor. Blend it until it becomes silky smooth, then transfer it to a mixing bowl.

Now add the crystallised pineapple and blanched almonds to the blended cheese with the essence and sugar to taste.

Prepare the flower pot by lining it with damp muslin. Put in the muslin so it drapes over the edge of the pot and a little way down the sides. Now pour in the cheese mixture, fold the spare muslin in over the top and then weight it down with a saucer and a 1 lb (450 g) weight. Then put it on a soup plate and leave in the fridge for a minimum of 12 hours to drain and compress. To serve, turn it out on to a serving plate, a stemmed one would be nice.

Top to bottom: Pashka; Cold Poached Eggs with Watercress Mayonnaise page 24, Mariner's Eggs page 26.

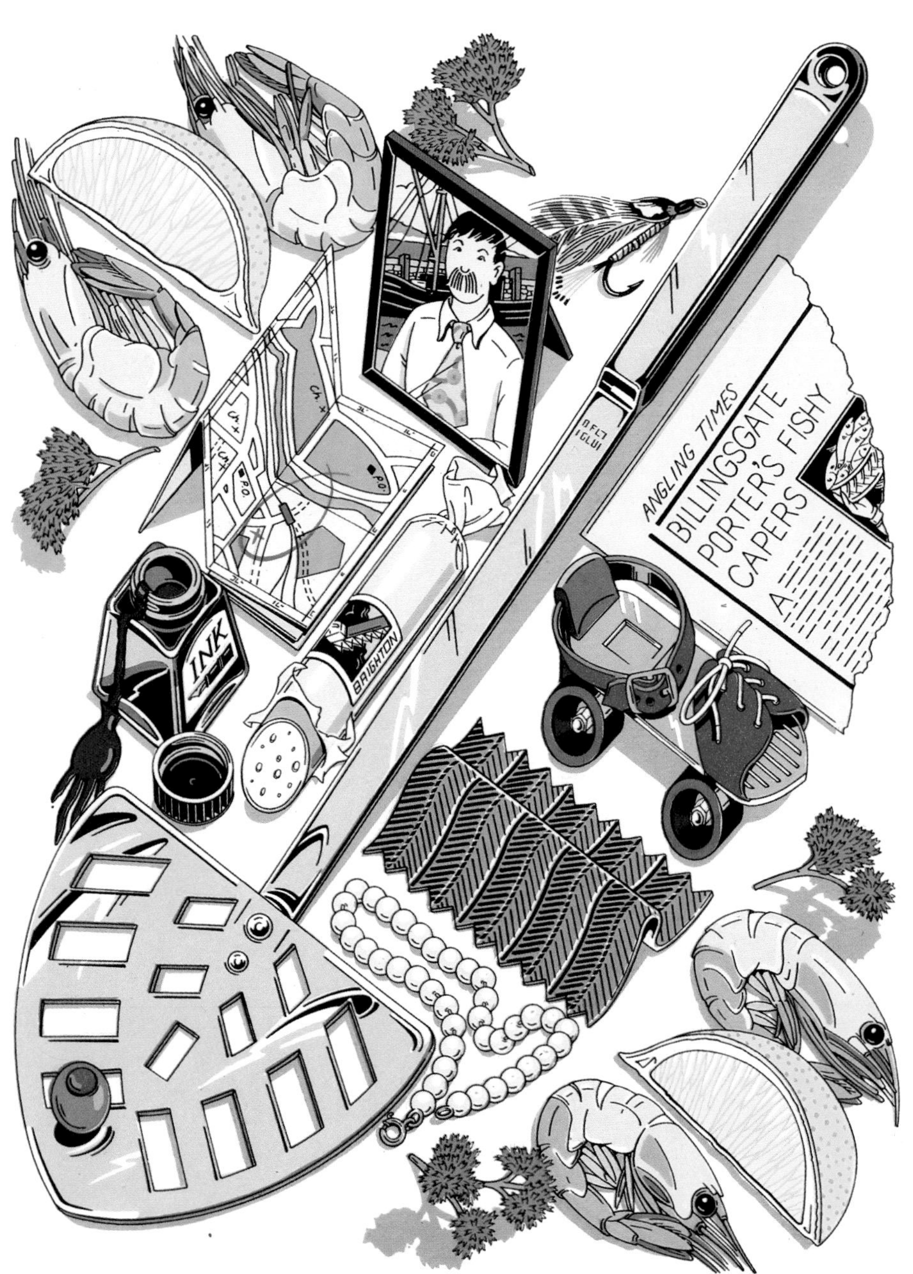
ANGLING TIMES
BILLINGSGATE PORTER'S FISHY CAPERS
INK
BRIGHTON

FISH

Kebabs of Prawns and Scallops with White Wine Sauce

Recipe sent by Molly Roberts Ballyconneely Co Galway

Serves 4–6 people

This recipe comes from the beautiful county of Galway in Ireland where the scallops and prawns are plump and plentiful. We like it served with a side salad and lots of crusty bread and Irish butter!

12 small or 6 large scallops
½ pint (275 ml) fish stock (see page 186)
1 clove garlic (skinned and crushed)
1 bayleaf
Salt and freshly-milled black pepper
36 cooked prawns (in their shells)
2 oz (50 g) butter
2 level tablespoons flour
¼ pint (150 ml) milk
¼ pint (150 ml) dry white wine
1 tablespoon wine vinegar
½ tablespoon tarragon
2 teaspoons chopped parsley

Pre-heat oven to gas mark 3, 325°F (170°C).

First place the scallops in a saucepan with the stock and simmer them gently for 4 minutes. Then drain and set the scallops aside. Now add the garlic, bayleaf and seasoning to the stock and boil briskly for 15 minutes without covering – it needs to be well reduced. Next strain the stock into a jug.

Now prepare the kebabs. If you are using large scallops then halve them and arrange the prawns and scallops on 4–6 skewers – allowing 3 prawns to every scallop. Then place the skewers in a large ovenproof dish or baking tray.

Using the same saucepan, melt the butter and add the flour and cook for 2 minutes until smooth and glossy. Gradually add the milk and fish stock and cook until thickened. Finally add the wine, vinegar, tarragon and parsley and taste to check the seasoning. Then pour the sauce over the kebabs and bake in the oven for about 20 minutes or until hot and bubbling. Serve them immediately and don't forget to provide some finger bowls.

Charles Dance's Prawns with Lemon and Garlic

Recipe sent by Charles Dance

Serves 2 people

This is one of Charles' favourite supper dishes, cooked by his wife Joanna, who recommended an accompaniment of some really nice chilled white wine and lots of crusty bread to mop up the buttery oil and lemon juices.

12 king prawns in their shells (¾ lb or 350 g)
4 fl. oz (110 ml) olive oil
Juice of 1 large lemon and grated zest of ½ a lemon
2 cloves of garlic (crushed)
1 teaspoon salt
Coarsely ground black pepper
2 oz (50 g) butter

First of all, line a grill pan with foil, then arrange the prawns in their shells on the foil.

Next, in a jug, mix together the oil, lemon juice, zest, crushed garlic and salt and pepper. Whisk everything together with a fork and then pour this mixture over the prawns. Leave them to marinate for at least an hour.

When you are ready to cook them, pre-heat the grill to a medium heat and then dot the butter over the prawns. Place them about 3 inches (7.5 cm) from the heat and grill, turning them frequently (tongs are useful for this). Cook them for about 5 or 6 minutes in all or until the skin darkens and begins to look slightly brown.

Serve on warm plates with the hot juices poured over and have some napkins and finger bowls on the table.

Krishna Spiced Prawns

Serves 4 people

Recipe sent by
A Barrie Crawford
East Kilbride
Glasgow

This is a delightful combination of flavours and is so quick to prepare. The spicy sauce does wonders for frozen prawns but freshly cooked peeled prawns would be particularly good.

1 lb (450 g) cooked peeled prawns
3 tablespoons oil
2 medium onions (finely chopped)
½ level teaspoon chilli powder
½ level teaspoon tumeric
1 level teaspoon ground coriander
1 level teaspoon brown sugar
4 cloves
2 inch (5 cm) piece cinnamon stick
2 teaspoons grated fresh root ginger
3 bayleaves
Salt
4 tomatoes (skinned and chopped)
2 inch (5 cm) cube creamed coconut

Heat the oil in a large frying-pan and gently fry the onions until golden brown, about 6 minutes. Add all the spices, sugar, bayleaves and seasonings and mix everything very well together for a minute or two, allowing the heat to draw out the flavours. After that add the tomatoes and bring these up to simmering point. Now stir in the prawns and cook these for 5 minutes, stirring all the time to coat with the spicy mixture.

Now turn the heat to a very gentle simmer and crumble the creamed coconut into the mixture. Stir until the coconut has dissolved and serve with rice and mango chutney.

Ken Lo's South Sea Noodles

Serves 3 – 4 people

Recipe sent by Kenneth Lo

Chinese noodle dishes are a great favourite with me, and I love the light rice noodles which soak up all the flavours, but Ken says that if these are not available in your area you can use spaghetti (cooked, drained and cooled under cold running water) for this instead. Also if you can't get dried shrimps – which are available in all Chinese shops – you can use extra fresh prawns.

10 oz (275 g) Chinese rice flour vermicelli (rice noodles) or spaghetti
2 tablespoons mild Chinese dried shrimps
2 medium onions (thinly sliced)
5 oz (150 g) salt pork or 4 rashers of bacon, cut into matchstick lengths
2 tablespoons mild curry powder
8 – 9 tablespoons strong chicken stock
4 tablespoons vegetable oil (not sesame)
½ teaspoon salt

For the garnish
8 oz (225 g) shelled prawns
2 cloves of garlic (finely chopped)
4 spring onions (cut into ½ inch or 1 cm lengths)
1 tablespoon soy sauce
1½ tablespoons hoisin sauce
2 tablespoons dry sherry
2 tablespoons vegetable oil
2 tablespoons fresh chopped parsley

Soak the dried shrimps in water for 20 minutes or so then drain them and chop them up small. Now blanch the noodles for 3 minutes in boiling water, then drain and rinse them under cold running water and leave in a colander to drain.

For the noodle sauce, heat the oil in a large pan (or wok) then add the onion, bacon and chopped dried shrimps. Stir-fry everything for 2 minutes before adding the curry powder and salt, then continue to stir-fry for another 1½ minutes.

Next heat the stock in a saucepan and pour this over the sauce ingredients and stir well. When it has started to bubble, add the drained noodles, stir and toss them around the pan until heated through – about 2 – 3 minutes. Then transfer the whole lot to a heated serving dish to keep warm.

For the garnish, heat the oil in a small pan, add the peeled prawns and garlic and stir-fry them over a high heat for 1 minute before adding the soy and hoisin sauces and sherry. Continue to stir-fry for 1 more minute, then sprinkle with the chopped spring onions and parsley. Turn the mixture a few times, pour it on top of the noodles and serve straightaway.

Note: for variety and a more substantial dish you can add ¼ lb (110 g) crabmeat or mushrooms to the garnish at the same time as the prawns. Or add ¼ lb (110 g) shredded Cos lettuce or bean sprouts just after the soy sauce has been stirred in.

Smoked Salmon Quiche

Recipe sent by
Mrs E Rowley
Droitwich Spa
Worcestershire

Serves 4 people or 6 as a starter

If you live near a smoked salmon supplier then the best choice for this is the small pieces of smoked salmon called 'off cuts'. If not, then the frozen slices of smoked salmon will do well.

Shortcrust pastry made with
4 oz (110 g) plain flour
2 oz (50 g) fat – 1 oz (25 g) butter and 1 oz (25 g) lard
A pinch of salt
A little water

For the filling
3 oz (75 g) smoked salmon (cut into small pieces)
2 eggs
½ pint (275 ml) cream (double or single)
1 teaspoon lemon juice
Salt and freshly-milled black pepper

To garnish
A few prawns
A few sprigs of watercress
Cayenne pepper

Pre-heat oven to gas mark 4, 350°F (180°C).

First of all make up the pastry and line an 8 inch (20 cm) metal quiche or flan tin with it. Prick all over with a fork and pre-bake it blind on a baking tray for 10 minutes in the centre of the oven. Then remove it and leave aside until the pastry has cooled a little.

Now line the pastry case with the salmon (leaving as few gaps as possible) and sprinkle the salmon with a little lemon juice. Then whisk together the eggs, cream and seasoning, then pour this mixture over the smoked salmon in the pastry case. Bake on a baking sheet in the centre of the oven for 40 minutes.

Serve either warm or cold garnished with prawns, watercress and a sprinkling of cayenne pepper.

Bruce Oldfield's Rosti with Smoked Salmon

Serves 4 people

Recipe sent by Bruce Oldfield

Bruce says he chose this because it's so 'quick and easy to prepare after a hard day's work'. It's also deliciously different.

2 lb (900 g) potatoes
4 oz (110 g) smoked salmon
1 dessertspoon lemon juice
2 tablespoons fresh chopped parsley
1½ tablespoons olive oil
Salt and cayenne pepper

First of all peel the potatoes and place them in a saucepan with enough water to cover, add some salt and boil them for exactly 7 minutes. After that drain them and place them on a plate until they're cool enough to handle.

Meanwhile use a sharp knife to cut the smoked salmon into smallish shreds, place them in a mixing bowl and toss them in the lemon juice.

When the potatoes are cool, grate them using the coarse side of the grater and add them to the smoked salmon along with the parsley. Mix everything together well (but gently, so that the grated potato doesn't break up).

Now heat the oil in a 9 inch (23 cm) heavy frying-pan (preferably non-stick) and as soon as it's hot tip the potato mixture into the pan. Turn the heat to very low, then spread the mixture out evenly using a palette knife or spatula. Sprinkle the surface with a little salt and a dusting of cayenne, then weight the potato down with a plate that fits nicely inside the pan, and cook gently for about 20 minutes. Turn out on to a warmed serving plate and serve cut into wedges.

Smokie Mousse

Recipe sent by
James Harvey
Glasgow
Scotland

Serves 4–6 people

Arbroath smokies are some of Scotland's finest smoked fish, and are superb made into a soft creamy mousse. If you are not lucky enough to be able to buy them in your area then you could use cooked smoked Finnan haddock.

1 pair Arbroath smokies (¾ – 1 lb or 350–450 g)
¼ pint (150 ml) good quality thick mayonnaise
¼ pint (150 ml) whipping cream
3 tablespoons water
½ oz (10 g) powdered gelatine (1 sachet)
2 egg whites
2 teaspoons lemon juice
Freshly-milled black pepper

You will need a 2 pint (1.25 litre) dish or 6 individual ramekin dishes.

First put the water in a small bowl and sprinkle the gelatine over it. Leave it for a few minutes to soften, then stand the bowl in a pan of hot water until the gelatine is completely dissolved and becomes transparent. Then leave it to cool.

Meanwhile, remove all the flesh from the smokies and flake it (Arbroath smokies are already cooked when bought). Then fold the flaked fish into the mayonnaise. After that whip the cream lightly (it should be thick and floppy but not stiff) and fold it into the mayonnaise. Lastly stir in the cooled gelatine and mix well.

Leave it until it is just beginning to set, about 5 minutes. Beat the egg whites to stiff peaks, then stir 1 tablespoon of the stiffly whisked egg whites into the fish mixture, season with freshly-milled black pepper and add the lemon juice. Then lightly fold in the rest of the egg whites.

Pour this mixture into a 2 pint (1.25 litre) dish or into

6 individual ramekin dishes, cover and chill in the refrigerator for several hours and serve with fingers of brown bread and butter or toast.

Scandinavian Spiced Herrings

Recipe sent by Janet Laurence Somerton Somerset

Serves 6 as a starter or 4 as a main course

This is one of my own special favourites and the author recommends that it be served as a starter with yoghurt or soured cream mixed with chopped chives or spring onions, and rye or pumpernickel bread. Or as a main course with new potatoes, hard-boiled eggs and a beetroot salad.

2 lb (900 g) very fresh herrings (block filleted)
1¾ pints (1 litre) water
6 fl. oz (175 ml) wine vinegar
6 oz (175 g) Barbados brown sugar
1½ tablespoons fine sea salt
1½ tablespoons whole allspice berries (crushed)
1½ tablespoons white peppercorns (crushed)
10 – 15 bayleaves

If the fishmonger won't block fillet the herrings, which means leaving the fish in one piece, you can take out the bones by opening up the belly, removing the guts and cleaning if necessary, then pressing the fish down on a board. Have the fish open, backbone against the work surface, and really work at pushing the flesh against the board along the backbone. You should then be able to ease the bone away from the flesh, together with most of the smaller bones. Try and leave the flesh as intact as possible. The fresher the fish, the more the bones will cling. Recalcitrant bones can be removed after the preliminary soaking. Lastly, cut off the small fins.

Now place the fish, opened out, in a deep dish that will hold them nicely (an oval dish of about 4 – 6 pints or 2.5 – 3.5 litres is most suitable). Add the water mixed with the vinegar; it should cover the fish completely. Leave in a cool place for about 3 hours.

Then take out the herrings, rinse in clean water and drain them well. Any large bones still in the herrings can be pulled out easily.

Next mix together the sugar, salt, allspice and peppercorns. The spices should not be reduced to a powder but should have lots of texture. Place a layer of spice mixture in the cleaned dish. Add 2 bayleaves and a layer of opened-out herring, skin side down. Add another layer of spice mixture and bayleaves. Place more herring, flesh side down, on top and repeat layers of spice and fish until all the fish is used up, ending with a layer of spice and bayleaves. Place a piece of tin foil on top, pressed down lightly, cover with a lid or more foil and put the dish in a cool place for 5–9 hours, depending on the size of the fish.

At the end of marinating time, remove the herrings and carefully wipe off any bits of flavourings adhering to the fish with dampened kitchen paper. Then remove any remaining largish bones or fins and trim the edges. The fish can be wrapped in clingfilm and kept in the fridge for several days, it will taste better the day after being made and will continue maturing nicely for another 2 or 3 days, or deep frozen for several months.

To serve, fold the fish back together and cut in ½ inch (1 cm) slices, slightly obliquely. Place on a dish, garnish with lemon and any of the accompaniments suggested above.

Polyglot Squid

Serves 4 people

Recipe sent by
Tony Wren
Stoke Newington
London N16

Served with rice, this is a very highly rated recipe among the FOOD AID team, but, if squid is not to your liking, then Tony Wren says it works extremely well with monkfish cut into cubes. If you use monkfish you should take the fish out after the initial frying and replace it when the sauce is half reduced.

2 lb (900 g) squid
1 lb (450 g) red ripe tomatoes
3 tablespoons olive oil
3 cloves garlic (peeled and chopped)
½ pint (275 ml) red wine (full-bodied from a hot country!)
1 rounded teaspoon dried basil (or 1 tablespoon of fresh if available)
1 teaspoon coriander seeds (crushed with seeds from 4 cardamom pods)

¼ teaspoon ground mace
4 oz (110 g) mushrooms (sliced)
3 tablespoons quark (or soured cream if unavailable)
Salt and freshly-milled black pepper

To serve
1 dessertspoon lemon juice
Sprinkling of fresh chopped herbs

First, peel the speckled skin off the squid and pull out the contents of the bag, discarding all save the tentacles. Remove the celluloid bit (quill) and discard it too. Then slice the bag (body) into rings.

Peel the tomatoes by dunking them into boiling water for 3 to 4 minutes. Slip off the skins and chop the flesh roughly.

Next heat the oil in a large, heavy frying-pan and fry the squid rings and tentacles until they turn opaque and slightly golden (5 minutes). Now add the peeled chopped tomatoes and garlic, then when they begin to soften add the wine and spices and simmer uncovered for 20 minutes. Then add the mushrooms and cook for 10 – 15 minutes more or until the squid is tender.

Bring everything up to simmering point and add the basil and spices and a seasoning of salt and freshly-milled black pepper. Simmer gently for a further 10 minutes and finally stir in the quark (or soured cream) just before serving. Serve with rice and sprinkle with lemon juice and herbs.

Scottish Oatmeal Stuffed Trout

Serves 4 people

Recipe sent by
Kate Hunter
Blairgowrie
Perthshire

I suspect that in Blairgowrie fresh wild trout is probably quite plentiful. However, those who can only get the farmed variety will find that Kate Hunter's recipe will make the fish much more special.

4 fresh trout
4 heaped tablespoons medium oatmeal
1 level tablespoon freshly chopped parsley
2 oz (50 g) butter
1 teaspoon vegetable oil

Grated rind of half a lemon
1 small onion (chopped finely)
1 clove garlic (crushed)
2 hard boiled eggs (chopped)
1 oz (25 g) shelled walnuts (chopped)
1 teaspoon tarragon leaves (chopped)
Salt and freshly-milled black pepper
1 heaped tablespoon mayonnaise

To cook
Little melted butter

To garnish
Lemon wedges
Parsley sprigs

Pre-heat oven to gas mark 5, 375 °F (190 °C).

Ask the fishmonger to de-head and bone the trout. Alternatively, chop off the heads and tails and, using kitchen scissors, cut right along the stomachs to the tails. To remove the backbones, place the fish flesh-side down on a board and press your thumb firmly along the skin, over the backbone to loosen them. Turn the fish over and carefully ease the bones out and remove any other visible bones.

Melt the butter and oil in a pan and sweat the onion and garlic until they are translucent, for about 5 minutes, then add the oatmeal and stir over the heat for a couple of minutes. Remove the pan from the heat and leave the mixture to cool. Add the rest of the ingredients, season well and stir everything together.

Spread an equal amount of stuffing on one side of each trout fillet, then ease the other side back over to re-shape the trout. To keep everything intact you can either tie each one with string or secure them with cocktail sticks. Now place the trout in a well-greased baking dish, brush each one with melted butter, cover loosely with a sheet of foil and bake for 30 minutes. Serve garnished with a sprig of parsley and a lemon wedge.

Baked Trout with Smoked Trout Stuffing

Serves 6 people

Recipe sent by
Sîan Cook
Tadley,
Hampshire

We are enormously grateful to Mrs Sîan Cook for such a lovely, simple, but original idea. She suggests a 3 lb (1 kg 350 g) trout for 6 people but as we were unable to locate one we made it with smaller trout and were delighted with the results.

6 × 7 oz (200 g) trout (cleaned and gutted)
6 oz (175 g) smoked trout or 1 × 8 oz (225 g) smoked trout before skinning and boning
2 oz (50 g) wholemeal breadcrumbs
2 tablespoons parsley (finely chopped)
Juice of ½ lemon
3 teaspoons creamed horseradish
2 egg yolks
1 tablespoon cream
1½ oz (40 g) melted butter or margarine
Salt and freshly-milled black pepper

For the garnish
6 lemon wedges
Watercress

Pre-heat oven to gas mark 5, 375°F (190°C).

First of all grease 6 rectangles of foil with the melted fat. Then flake the smoked trout into a mixing bowl and mix it with the breadcrumbs and parsley.

In another bowl beat the lemon juice, creamed horseradish and egg yolks together, then add the cream and stir this mixture into the other stuffing ingredients. Mix everything well, taste and check the seasoning then carefully fill each trout with the stuffing, then brush each one with melted fat. Wrap them up into neat parcels and seal the edges to prevent the juices escaping.

Now arrange the parcels on a large baking sheet and bake in the oven for exactly 30 minutes. Serve the trout with the juices poured over, garnished with lemon wedges and watercress. Tiny new potatoes and the *Polish Cucumber Salad* (page 125) would be a perfect accompaniment.

Punjabi Baked Fish in Mint Sauce

Serves 4 people

Recipe sent by
Bina Sawhney
Leighton Buzzard
Bedfordshire

This is a very beautiful and unusual recipe and one that proves it is not always necessary to spend hours in the kitchen to produce something exotic.

4 large steaks or fillets of any white fish (weighing about 1½ lb or 700 g in all)
4 cloves garlic (skinned and crushed)
1 inch piece of ginger (peeled and grated)
1 teaspoon coriander powder
Salt and freshly-milled black pepper
Oil for frying

For the sauce
15 – 20 fresh mint leaves
1 hot green chilli
1 tablespoon fresh lime or lemon juice
4 tablespoons tomato purée
3 tablespoons water

Pre-heat oven to gas mark 3, 325 °F (170 °C).

First of all, using a pestle and mortar, crush the garlic with a little salt to make a creamy paste, then add the ginger, coriander powder and freshly-milled black pepper. Rub this mixture into the fish steaks and leave them covered on a plate for 15 minutes.

Meanwhile make the sauce. This you do by finely chopping the mint leaves and the chilli (remove the seeds from the chilli unless you like it really hot!). Then place the chilli and the mint in a small saucepan with the lime or lemon juice, tomato purée and water, then heat this very gently for 3 minutes, stirring to mix everything well.

Next, heat 2 tablespoons of oil in a flameproof casserole large enough to hold the fish in a single layer. When this is hot, fry the pieces of fish for 2 minutes on each side, skin side first, and then pour the sauce over the fish, cover with a lid and transfer to the oven for 15 minutes. Serve this with pilau rice or Indian chapattis.

Left: Punjabi Baked Fish in Mint Sauce. Right: Fricassée of Monkfish with Fresh Lime and Ginger *page 51.*

Lady Booth's Gratin of Fresh Haddock

Serves 3 people

Recipe sent by
Lady Booth
Solihull
West Midlands

Taken from the hot grill this looks like fish in a cream cheese sauce but underneath there's a hidden tomato sauce and these two sauces together really complement the fish.

1 lb (450 g) fresh haddock
5 oz (150 g) French shallots (finely chopped)
4 oz (110 g) tomatoes (peeled and chopped)
4 oz (110 g) sharp Cheddar cheese (grated)
½ pint (275 ml) milk
¼ pint (150 ml) dry white wine or cider
1 oz (25 g) plain flour
2½ oz (60 g) butter
1 teaspoon dried sweet basil
1 clove garlic (crushed)
Salt and freshly-milled black pepper

To serve
1 tablespoon chopped parsley

First of all, place the haddock in a saucepan with the milk, add some salt and freshly-milled black pepper and poach the haddock gently for about 7 minutes. Strain off all the liquid into a jug. Remove the skin from the fish and divide it into flakes, reserving it in the saucepan.

Next, make a sauce by melting 1½ oz (40 g) of the butter in the saucepan. Add the flour, stir and cook for 3 minutes to get it really smooth, then begin to add the milk that the fish was cooked in a little at a time, stirring continually until it has all been incorporated and you have a smooth sauce. Add the wine, a little at a time, and continue to whisk until smooth. Taste to check the seasoning, lower the heat, then stir in the flaked fish and all the cheese, except for 1 tablespoon, and cook gently for a further 3 minutes. After that pre-heat the grill to its highest setting.

In a frying pan melt the remaining butter and add the chopped shallots and crushed garlic. Cook for 5 minutes, then add the tomatoes and basil, season with salt and freshly-milled black pepper and simmer for a further 5 minutes.

Spoon the tomato mixture into the base of a buttered gratin or baking dish, then pour the fish mixture on top and finally sprinkle the surface with the rest of the cheese. Then place the dish under the hot grill for about 5 minutes or until the surface is browned and bubbling. Sprinkle over the chopped parsley before serving. Lady Booth recommends new potatoes and mangetout as suitable accompaniments.

Fricassée of Monkfish with Fresh Lime and Ginger

Recipe sent by
Graham Tinsley
Warrington
Cheshire

Serves 4 people

Here speed and simplicity are combined to produce a beautiful dish out of a few ingredients – although this one did come from a professional chef!

1½ lb (700 g) monkfish (boned and skinned – ask the fishmonger to do this for you)
8 fl. oz (225 ml) double cream
2 oz (50 g) butter
Grated zest and juice of 2 fresh limes
1 oz (25 g) finely grated fresh root ginger
Salt and freshly-milled black pepper
Cayenne pepper

For the garnish
4 oz (110 g) each of carrots, courgettes and turnips (all of them cut into thin 2 inch (5 cm) strips, ¼ inch (5 mm) thick)
1 teaspoon butter

The idea of this recipe is to serve the fish on a bed of colourful strips of vegetables: these should be *al dente* (that is, cooked but still crisp to bite). The best way to achieve this is to have ready a 4½ pint (2.5 litre) saucepan three-quarters full of simmering salted water. Then while you are making the sauce for the fish, drop the prepared vegetables into the boiling water, bring back to the boil and then simmer for exactly 2 minutes: drain them in a colander and cover with a cloth to keep warm.

First, then, cut the monkfish into fine goujons (little strips about 1½ inches (4 cm) long and ¼ inch (5 mm) wide). Season them with salt, freshly-milled pepper and a couple of pinches of cayenne. Now heat the butter in a large frying pan, and when it begins to foam add the pieces of monkfish, tossing them gently around the pan.

When they all have a nice pale golden colour, remove them from the pan and keep warm. Next, add the fresh lime juice and zest and grated ginger to the pan and stir them around to distribute evenly and mix with the butter in the pan.

At this stage pop the prepared vegetables into the pan of boiling water (see above), and then return to the sauce. Pour the cream into the lime juice mixture and mix well, then continue to cook until it has reduced to a good sauce consistency. Taste and season as required and return the fish to the sauce.

Melt a knob of butter in a pan and toss the drained strips of vegetable in it to give a nice glaze, then arrange them on 4 warmed plates. Spoon the fish on to each base of vegetables, coat it with the sauce and serve immediately.

Pepper Fish Parcels with Avocado Sauce

Recipe sent by
Julio Grau
Birmingham

Serves 4–6 people

This is an unusual but very simple way of cooking fish. Serve it for 4 with rice as a supper dish or for 6 as a first course.

For the fish
2 red peppers
2 yellow peppers (green discolour on steaming)
1½ lb (700 g) firm white fish (monkfish, sole or plaice)
Oil
Salt
Cayenne pepper
A little butter

For the sauce
1 avocado
2 fl. oz (55 ml) water and 3 fl. oz (75 ml) white wine
Salt
Cayenne pepper
1 teaspoon lemon juice

Pre-heat oven to gas mark 9, 475°F (240°C).

First make the sauce, which is very simple. All you do is scoop the flesh out of the avocado, chop it into small pieces and place it in a small saucepan. Scrape the avocado skin to get every last bit of flesh as this is the greenest part and helps colouring. Now add the water and wine to the avocado and simmer it for 10 minutes. Then transfer it to a liquidiser and blend until smooth, season with salt and cayenne pepper, add the lemon juice and return it to the saucepan.

Now for the fish. Brush the peppers lightly with oil, then place them on a baking sheet and bake in the oven for 15 minutes, turning them over occasionally until the skin is blackened all over. Then leave them to cool before peeling off the black skin and discarding the seeds. Cut each pepper in half, and then each half into 3 slices lengthways.

Now cut the fish into 12 even-sized pieces and season well. Place a piece of fish on a slice of pepper, add a dot of butter and cover with another colour pepper slice. Then do the same with all the fish and pepper pieces.

Steam the fish either between 2 deep plates or in a steamer over a large pan of boiling water for about 5 minutes (thick pieces of monkfish may take about 7 minutes). Serve 2 or 3 parcels per person with the sauce poured over them.

Moli (Burmese Spiced Fish in Coconut)

Recipe sent by
Fiona Ruffles
East Dulwich
London SE22

Serves 2 people

This delightfully unusual fish dish cannot take much more than 20 minutes from start to finish. Fiona Ruffles recommended that it is served with brown rice and a cucumber and tomato salad.

2 × 8 oz (225 g) cod steaks or fillets
2 tablespoons groundnut oil
1 medium onion (finely chopped)
1 green chilli (de-seeded and finely chopped)
1 large or 2 small cloves garlic (crushed)
½ teaspoon ground tumeric
3 oz (75 g) creamed coconut
½ pint (275 ml) hot water
1 level teaspoon salt
The juice of 1 lime or ½ lemon

This can be made in a small frying-pan.

Start off by heating the oil and frying the onion in it for 5 minutes. Then add the chilli, garlic and tumeric and continue to fry for a further 5 minutes or until the onion begins to turn golden brown at the edges. Then place the fish steaks in this mixture, cook for a minute or two and then turn over – this is to give each one a nice coating of the spiced onion mixture. If your fish is a fillet rather than a steak, then place it flesh side in first and then turn it over.

Now put the creamed coconut into a jug and pour the hot water over it and whisk with a large fork to dissolve it. Then pour this over the fish and simmer it without covering for 10 – 15 minutes or until the fish is cooked.

Finally, sprinkle in the salt and lime juice. If the lime is very juicy and the sauce looks too thin let it bubble and reduce a little. Then serve the fish with the sauce poured over.

Jeffrey Archer's Creamed Seafood Bake

Serves 4 – 6 people

Recipe sent by Jeffrey Archer

The fish you use for this can be any mixture you like – fresh crab, king prawns, scallops, etc. It makes a beautiful supper dish for six, or four greedy people, and it doesn't need any last-minute preparation.

For the rice

Long grain brown rice measured to the ½ pint (275 ml) level in a glass measuring jug
1 pint (570 ml) boiling water
1 dessertspoon oil
½ onion (finely chopped)
3 oz (75 g) golden raisins or sultanas

For the rest of the ingredients

1½ lb (700 g) seafood (we used 8 oz or 225 g each of prawns, halibut, skinned and cut into chunks, and scallops, sliced)
4 oz (110 g) butter
4 oz (110 g) mushrooms (sliced)
3 fl. oz (75 ml) dry sherry
1 oz (25 g) plain flour
2 teaspoons fresh root ginger (peeled and grated)

2 teaspoons hot curry powder
½ teaspoon mustard powder
½ pint (275 ml) single cream
4 oz (110 g) Cheddar cheese (grated)
Cayenne pepper
Salt and freshly-milled black pepper

Pre-heat oven to gas mark 6, 400°F (200°C).
You'll also need a buttered baking dish measuring 8 by 12 inches (20 by 30 cm) and 2 inches (5 cm) deep.

First cook the rice by heating the oil in a medium-sized saucepan and adding the onion. Cook for 5 minutes or so to soften, then add the rice and raisins (or sultanas) and stir them around to get them coated with oil. Now pour in the boiling water, stir once, then cover the pan and leave to cook over a very gentle heat for 40 minutes, or until all the liquid has been absorbed and the grains are tender.

While the rice is cooking you can be preparing the filling. Melt 2 oz (50 g) of the butter in a large frying-pan and sauté the mushrooms for 2–3 minutes, then remove them with a draining spoon and keep them on one side in a dish. Now add another 1 oz (25 g) of butter to the pan and when it has melted add the halibut pieces and the sliced scallops together with the sherry. Cook for 4–5 minutes, keeping the heat at medium, then transfer the fish to join the mushrooms in the dish. Pour the juices from the pan into a jug.

Next add the final 1 oz (25 g) of butter to the pan, and when melted stir in the flour till smooth and add the ginger, curry powder and mustard. Now gradually stir in the reserved fish liquid and the cream and when it has thickened, pour the sauce over the fish and mushrooms. Add the prawns then mix everything together, taste and season well.

Arrange the rice in the base of the buttered baking dish, spoon the fish mixture over that, sprinkle the surface with the grated cheese and a dusting of cayenne. Bake in the oven for 30 minutes or until the top is brown and bubbling.

Gratin of Seafood with Garlic Crumble

Recipe sent by Patsy Major Leigh-on-Sea Essex

Serves 4 people

You can choose almost any variety of fish for this – cod, haddock, skate or even squid. It's deliciously creamy and the crumble topping makes this very much nicer than a fish pie made with an ordinary pastry topping.

1¼ lb (550 g) various fish (see above), skinned and filleted
¼ lb (110 g) peeled prawns
¾ pint (425 ml) milk
2 bayleaves
A pinch of powdered mace
1½ oz (40 g) butter
1½ oz (40 g) flour
1 tablespoon lemon juice
1 small onion (chopped)
½ green pepper (chopped)
1 tablespoon capers (drained)
1 tablespoon fresh chopped parsley
1 tablespoon oil
Salt and freshly-milled black pepper

For the topping
4 oz (110 g) breadcrumbs
2 cloves of garlic (crushed)
2 oz (50 g) grated cheese
1 oz (25 g) butter (cut into small dice)
Salt and freshly-milled black pepper

Pre-heat oven to gas mark 5, 375°F (190°C).
You'll also need a 3 pint (1.7 litre) ovenproof baking dish.

Begin by placing the fish (not the prawns) in a heavy saucepan and pouring in the milk. Add the bayleaves, the mace and a seasoning of salt and pepper, then poach the fish lightly until barely cooked – about 6 minutes. Now remove the fish and strain the milk into a jug ready for the sauce.

Make up the sauce by melting the butter in the same saucepan (to save washing-up!), then stir in the flour. Now add the fish liquid and the lemon juice, a little at a time, stirring after each addition until you have a smooth sauce, then cook the sauce gently for 5 minutes.

Meanwhile heat the oil in a frying-pan and cook the onion

and green pepper in it until softened – about 10 minutes but be careful not to let them brown. Then remove them from the heat and leave on one side.

Next flake the fish (discarding any skin) and place it together with the prawns in the ovenproof baking dish. Add the onion and pepper plus the capers, then stir the parsley into the sauce and pour that all over the fish and vegetables.

Now for the crumble topping: mix the breadcrumbs, garlic, grated cheese and butter together, season, then sprinkle this over the top of the fish. Place the dish in the pre-heated oven and cook for approximately 20 minutes or until the top is golden brown. Serve with creamed potatoes as a main course, or with a green salad as a lunch or supper dish.

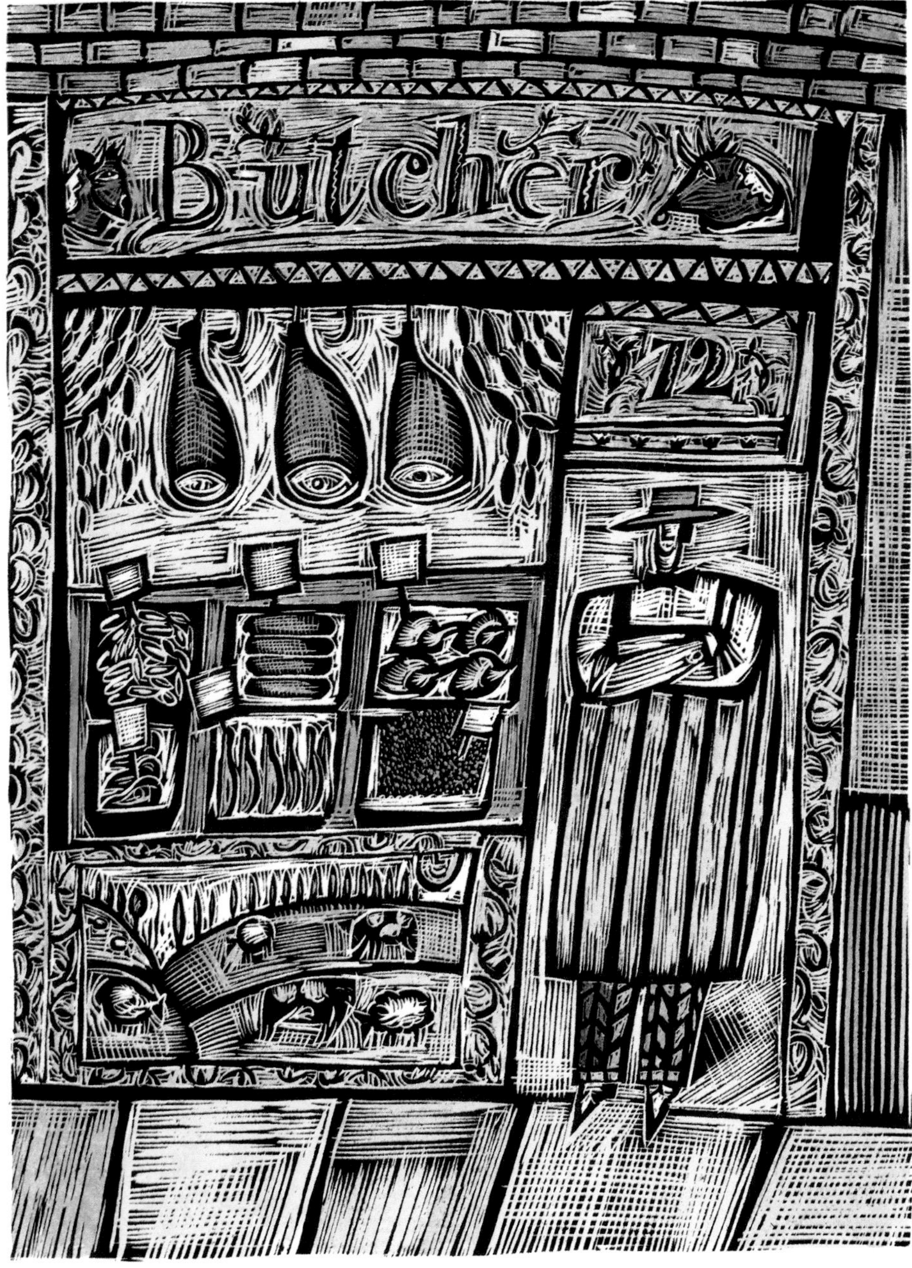
Butcher
72

MEAT

Beef in Guinness with Orange Sauce

Serves 4 – 6 people

Recipe sent by
Marion Shaw
Windsor
Berks

This recipe is one of those that truly tastes better if it is made the day before. Its long slow cooking produces a very rich, dark and fragrant sauce and is perfect for entertaining as it allows you to work so far in advance. Mrs Shaw recommends rump steak, but it also works well with any stewing beef cut.

2 lb (900 g) beef (cut into 2 inch or 5 cm cubes)
2 level tablespoons seasoned flour
3 oz (75 g) butter
1 medium onion (approx. 4 oz or 110 g, finely chopped)
2 cloves garlic (crushed)
4 oz (110 g) carrots (sliced thickly)
2 oz (50 g) turnips (cut into small chunks)
2 oz (50 g) celery (chopped)
A good grating of nutmeg
¼ teaspoon powdered allspice
1 bottle of Guinness (1 pint)
Salt and freshly-milled black pepper
Grated zest and juice of 2 oranges

To serve
Freshly chopped parsley

Pre-heat oven to gas mark ½, 250°F (130°C).
I used a large, heavy frying-pan for this together with a flameproof casserole.

Begin by putting 1 oz (25 g) of butter in the casserole and over a gentle heat sweat the onion and garlic in it for about 10 minutes. Heat the frying-pan and add another ounce (25 g) of butter.

Meanwhile, toss the cubes of meat in the seasoned flour and brown them a few at a time in the frying-pan in the hot butter, transferring them into the casserole to join the onions and garlic. When the meat is all in, do the same with the vegetables, adding a little more butter if you need to, browning them just a little at the corners and edges.

When they are all in the casserole, sprinkle in the spices, some salt and freshly-milled black pepper and pour in the Guinness – it will seem a little too much, but don't worry, the long, slow cooking will take care of it all. Next, bring it up to simmering point, then transfer it to the pre-heated oven, where you can happily abandon it for 6 hours.

After that, stir in the grated zest and juice of the oranges and allow it to cool. The next day re-heat it in a pre-heated oven gas mark 2, 300°F (150°C) for about 45 minutes. Serve with some creamy mashed potatoes, which will make a good contrast to the rich dark sauce, and sprinkle with some freshly chopped parsley.

Spiced Beef

For a 7 lb (3 kg) joint

Recipe sent by
Mrs E L Williamson
Fareham
Hampshire

'This recipe,' says Mrs Williamson, 'has been followed at Christmas in our family for as long as I can remember.' Certainly it's not an everyday recipe, not least because it takes a fortnight to spice the beef! But we can vouch for the fact that it *is* worth it for a special family occasion like Christmas. There is nothing difficult about it – you only have to remember to visit the beef regularly while it is being spiced.

7 lb (approx. 3 kg) joint of brisket of beef (with the bone in)
6 oz (175 g) salt
8 oz (225 g) soft brown sugar
1 oz (25 g) saltpetre (obtainable from chemists)
½ oz (10 g) white pepper
½ oz (10 g) ground allspice (for meat *not* the pudding spice)
1 teaspoon ground mace
1 teaspoon ground cloves
1 teaspoon freshly grated nutmeg

The best container for the beef while it is being spiced is in fact a plastic washing-up bowl, though if you have one you could use a preserving pan provided it's not brass. First the joint has to be salted, so rub the 6 oz (175 g) of salt all over it, then leave it in the bowl at the bottom of the fridge for 24 hours.

After that remove the meat, drain off the liquid from the bowl and rinse it out, then return the joint to the bowl. Now combine all the spices, sugar and saltpetre together, and rub this mixture all over the beef. Cover the bowl with foil and leave it in the bottom of the fridge for 12 days. You will need to turn the joint once or twice a day during that period, and baste it with the spicy, syrupy juices that will emerge.

When you are ready to cook it, place the meat in a large deep pan (along with the juices) and pour in sufficient cold water to cover it. Bring to the boil, then boil gently (uncovered) for 3 ½ hours. Then turn the heat off and leave the meat in the liquid for a further hour.

By then it should be cool enough to handle (otherwise leave it until it is!), then remove the bones. If you're lucky they might pull out, if not use a sharp knife to remove them.

Now you can either press the joint between two plates with a weight on the top one, or else roll it up, place it in a 6 inch diameter cake tin and perch a plate on top with a heavy scale weight on it. Leave it being pressed until it is absolutely cold – or even overnight – then serve it cut into thin slices, perhaps with jacket potatoes and chutney.

Ronnie Barker's Marinated Spare Ribs

Serves 6 as a starter or 2 – 3 as a main course

Recipe sent by Ronnie Barker

Do try to get really meaty ribs for this. After the marinating and long cooking the spicy meat almost falls off the bones. Luscious!

2 lb (900 g) spare ribs
5 tablespoons tomato purée
2 tablespoons clear honey
2 tablespoons soy sauce
3 tablespoons red wine vinegar
½ pint (275 ml) beef stock (or dry cider if you haven't any stock)
Salt and freshly-milled black pepper

Spread the ribs out evenly in a single layer in a large ovenproof dish, and season them lightly with salt and pepper. Then simply whisk all the remaining ingredients together with a fork and pour the mixture over the ribs, turning them over so that all sides of each rib are well coated. Now leave them in a cool place for about 3 hours, turning the ribs over in the marinade occasionally.

Pre-heat the oven to gas mark 6, 400°F (200°C). Roast the ribs in the marinade mixture for half an hour, basting them from time to time, then after that reduce the heat to gas mark 4, 350°F (180°C). Cover the dish with foil and continue to roast the ribs for a further 1 hour (still basting from time to time).

Serve them on their own as a first course, or with rice and a salad for a main course. *Note:* If the mixture looks a bit dry towards the end of the cooking time, add a couple of tablespoons of hot water.

Ronnie Barker's £5 Note Sandwich

Ronnie has also devised another interesting recipe for us, which we are printing as sent – and leave to you to test!

2 slices bread (brown)
1 envelope (brown, white or wholemeal to taste)
4 oz (110 g) ham
2 oz (50 g) cheese (grated)
1 dessertspoon mayonnaise
One £5 note
1 teaspoon Gentleman's Relish

Lightly butter the bread. Chop ham into small pieces. Fold the chopped ham and grated cheese into the mayonnaise, and spread on to one of the slices of bread. Place the other slice of bread on top and cut in half diagonally. Fold £5 note into envelope, whisk off to FOOD AID and eat the sandwich with relish, knowing that someone else will eat with the £5 note.

West African Groundnut Stew

Recipe sent by
Kim Yorkshire
Warlingham
Surrey

Serves 4 people

Two reactions seem to occur at the mention of peanut butter: either people's eyes glaze over in delight or there's a totally opposite response. But anyone who has been to Africa nearly always enthuses about this typical stew. Now at last I've tried it myself and can honestly say that the peanut butter provides a delicious sauce. Kim Yorkshire says it is also very popular with teenagers!

1 lb (450 g) stewing beef (cut into cubes)
6 tablespoons smooth peanut butter
2 medium onions (roughly chopped)
1 lb (450 g) ripe tomatoes (peeled and chopped) or a 14 oz (400 g) tin Italian chopped tomatoes
3 fresh chillies (the rounded triangular ones, not the long thin lethal sort!)
1 lb (450 g) carrots (or a mixture of carrots, turnips and courgettes to make up 1 lb (450 g))
Pinch of mixed herbs
1 inch (2.5 cm) piece of grated fresh root ginger or 1 heaped teaspoon dried ginger
Salt and freshly-milled black pepper

For the accompaniment
7 oz (200 g) black-eyed beans
7 fl. oz (200 ml) long grain rice (measured in a glass measuring jug)

This is all cooked on top of the stove in a very heavy saucepan with a tight fitting lid, as the meat needs to cook in its own juices, or a flameproof casserole. If you have a pressure cooker use it as an ordinary saucepan, as it seals in the steam beautifully. Also, if you are not sure of the fitting of your saucepan or casserole lid then use a double sheet of foil to line it and give it a more secure fit.

First, de-seed the chillies, discarding the seeds, and chop them finely and combine with the peanut butter, ginger, herbs, vegetables and tomatoes and mix well.

Place the meat in the saucepan or casserole, followed by the vegetable mixture and some seasoning. Put on a close fitting lid and cook very slowly on top of the stove for approximately 1½ hours or until meat is tender. Don't worry about the apparent lack of liquid because the meat and vegetables will provide enough.

The black-eyed beans need to be brought to the boil and soaked, off the heat, for one hour, then simmered gently for another hour. The rice is cooked in double its volume of salted water (14 fl. oz or 400 ml) for 15 to 20 minutes.

Before serving, season the beans with salt and freshly-milled black pepper and mix them in with the rice. Serve them as an accompaniment to the stew.

Chilli Meat Balls in Chilli Sauce

Recipe sent by
Peppi Neale
Muswell Hill
London N10

Serves 4 people

This is extremely good and much loved by seasoned chilli fans – the sender likes it really hot but for those with less robust taste she recommends using a mild chilli powder.

For the chilli meatballs
1 lb (450 g) finely minced beef
2 oz (50 g) breadcrumbs
1 large egg (beaten)
2 teaspoons chilli powder (see above)
1 medium onion (grated or very finely chopped)
2 tablespoons tomato juice (or 1 tablespoon tomato purée mixed with 1 tablespoon water)
1 teaspoon salt
Freshly-milled black pepper
3 tablespoons oil (for frying)

For the chilli sauce
1 onion (chopped)
1 green pepper (chopped)
3 teaspoons chilli powder (see above)
1 teaspoon oregano
2 cloves garlic (crushed)
1 × 8 oz (225 g) tin of Italian tomatoes
1 small tin red kidney beans (drained)
1 level teaspoon salt
Freshly-milled black pepper
1 tablespoon oil (for frying)

Pre-heat oven to gas mark 5, 375 °F (190 °C).

In a large mixing bowl simply mix together all the ingredients for the chilli meat balls, mixing everything thoroughly and evenly. Then roll the mixture into little rounds – you should get about 12 – 14 altogether.

Heat the oil in a frying-pan and, when it is hot, brown the meat balls on all sides. Using a draining spoon, remove them to a flameproof casserole.

Then make the sauce – heat the oil in a frying-pan, add the chopped onion and fry till transparent, about 5 – 8 minutes. Add the green pepper, chilli powder, oregano and 5 fl. oz (150 ml) of water. Simmer everything until the pepper feels softened – about 5 minutes. Then add the garlic, tinned tomatoes and kidney beans, together with 1 teaspoon salt and some freshly-milled black pepper. Then simmer for about 5 – 7 minutes or until it has reduced and thickened slightly.

Pour the sauce over the meat balls, bring everything up to simmering point on top of the stove and then transfer the casserole to the oven, and cook (uncovered) for a further 15 minutes. We served this with brown rice and a salad made with lettuce, watercress, sliced avocado and a garlic flavoured vinaigrette.

Fasoulia (Spicy Lamb and Bean Stew)

Serves 6 people

Recipe sent by
Elizabeth Bascal
Ramsgate
Kent

This is a good supper dish for a cold, wintery day, easy to make but you need to prepare it well in advance (at least 3 hours).

8 oz (225 g) medium-sized white haricot beans (not soaked)
1 large onion (roughly chopped)
4 large or 8 small pieces of neck of lamb (this can be best end of neck chops or middle of neck on the bone, a piece about 1½ lb or 700 g in all)
Olive oil for frying
5 oz (150 g) tin tomato purée
3 cloves garlic (crushed)
1 level teaspoon chilli powder (or more if you like it hotter)
1 heaped teaspoon tumeric
1 level teaspoon coriander
1 level teaspoon cinnamon
1 teaspoon salt

First wash the beans in cold water and then drain them and place in a large saucepan. To this add 4 pints (2.15 litres) of cold water and half the onion. Then place the saucepan on a low heat, allow the beans to come very slowly to the boil without a lid, then keeping to a very low heat leave the beans to cook slowly for 2 hours (still without a lid). The beans should now be partly cooked but still a bit on the tough side.

Next add the meat and salt; if the water does not cover the meat you can add a little more. Then leave for a further hour of slow simmering or until the meat is tender. After that heat the oil in a small saucepan and gently fry the remaining onion until very tender but not brown, about 6 minutes. Then add the tomato purée and garlic and stir until it fizzles, next add all the spices. Cook slowly, stirring all the time, for about 5 minutes.

At this stage check the beans. If there seems to be too much liquid, ladle some off and if too little, add a spot more. This is difficult to assess as it depends on how slowly you can actually cook it. Anyway, what you now need to do is add a ladle full of bean liquid to the spices, stir and transfer to the beans and meat and cook for a further 15 minutes or until the sauce is thick. Then taste and season before serving.

In Libya where the fasoulia is served they eat it with fresh French bread. But we like it with yoghurt and a little rice.

Roghan Josh

Recipe sent by
Mrs K Puri
Crosby
Merseyside

Serves 3 – 4 people

This is an authentic Indian dish of spiced lamb. We found neck fillet from the supermarket a perfect cut for it. Serve with spiced rice (see page 190), Indian chutney and pickles.

1 lb (450 g) lean boneless lamb, cut into bite-sized pieces
1 inch (2.5 cm) green root ginger
3 – 4 cloves garlic
2 oz (50 g) natural yoghurt
1 level teaspoon chilli powder
1 teaspoon salt
2 oz (50 g) unsalted butter
2 medium-sized onions (finely chopped)
1½ teaspoons turmeric powder
1 level teaspoon ground coriander
½ teaspoon cumin seeds
4 small cardamoms
4 oz (110 g) peeled tomatoes
1½ teaspoons garam masala
Freshly-milled black pepper
1 oz (25 g) ground almonds

First of all place the cubes of lamb in a bowl. Then peel and finely chop the fresh ginger root and the garlic. Mix together the yoghurt, chilli powder, salt, ginger and garlic and add this to the cubes of lamb. Mix everything well with a wooden spoon to coat the pieces of meat on all sides. Cover the bowl and leave in the fridge for 3 hours to marinate.

When you are ready to cook the curry, heat the butter in a pan and fry the finely chopped onions until evenly browned. Add the turmeric, coriander and cumin seeds and unfold the cardamom pods and add the seeds along with the skins, then add the peeled tomatoes. Now simmer this mixture over a medium heat for 2 – 3 minutes then add the cubes of lamb and its marinade, stirring and turning the meat constantly. Then sprinkle in half of the garam masala, some freshly-milled black pepper and 10 fl. oz (275 ml) of water.

Now bring everything to the boil, cover the pan and reduce the heat and cook at the gentlest heat possible for 35 – 40 minutes or until the lamb is tender.

Before serving the Roghan Josh, sprinkle on the remaining garam masala and ground almonds. Stir and serve at once.

Baked Lamb with Kiwi, Pernod and Mint

Recipe sent by
Dr Roger Banks
Sheffield

Serves 4 people

Dr Roger Banks may have missed his vocation as he sounds as if he could have been a very inventive and imaginative chef. However, I'm sure he is much appreciated in the medical field. When he serves this, he says, there are cries of 'ooh! ah! and good grief what is *that*?' We think it is very good.

2 neck of lamb fillets divided in half (ie 4 pieces)
1 tablespoon olive oil
1 oz (25 g) butter

For the salt crust
12 oz (350 g) flour
6 oz (175 g) salt
8 tablespoons water
2 egg whites

For the sauce
3 kiwi fruit (peeled and tough core removed)
1 level tablespoon chopped fresh mint
1 dessertspoon Pernod (or other aniseed-flavoured aperitif)

1 teaspoon lemon juice
Salt and freshly-milled black pepper

To garnish
Watercress

Pre-heat oven to gas mark 8, 450°F (230°C).

The meat is cooked in an inedible salt crust pastry which produces well-flavoured and beautifully juicy lamb. To prepare the salt crust pastry, combine the flour and salt and gradually add the 8 tablespoons of water then the egg whites. This can be done in a food processor or with an electric whisk.

The resulting dough should be quite firm; if it is too wet then add a little more flour. Wrap the dough in clingfilm and chill for an hour. Then divide the chilled dough into 4 pieces and roll each one out to about 8 inches (20 cm) square and ¼ inch (5 mm) in thickness.

Now heat the oil and butter in a frying-pan and when it is really hot brown the lamb pieces on all sides. Then drain each piece well and wrap it in a pastry square, sealing the edges with water and ensuring that there are no gaps in the pastry. Place the pastry parcels on a lightly oiled baking sheet. Now bake the lamb parcels in the pre-heated oven for 10–15 minutes, depending on how well-cooked you like your lamb to be.

Next, whilst the lamb is cooking, prepare the sauce. In a blender or food processor, combine the kiwi fruit, mint, Pernod and lemon juice. Taste, season and pour the mixture into a small saucepan.

Then remove the lamb from the oven, leave it for 5 minutes, and then break open the parcels over the saucepan to catch the juices. Heat the sauce gently while you slice the meat thinly. Then arrange the meat on a warmed plate, garnish with watercress, spoon the sauce around the lamb and serve.

Lamb Cutlets Shrewsbury

Serves 3 people

Recipe sent by
Stephen Grisby
Bristol

This is an easy and delightful recipe, especially good in the height of summer when lamb is at its best. It also works well with lean, trimmed loin chops but in this case you need to increase the cooking time to 40–45 minutes.

9 lamb cutlets from best end of neck (trim off any excess fat)
1 oz (25 g) dripping
4 oz (110 g) button mushrooms (trimmed and sliced finely)
4 tablespoons of a good quality redcurrant jelly
2 tablespoons Worcestershire sauce
Juice of 1 lemon
1 level tablespoon plain flour
¼ – ½ pint (150–275 ml) red wine
Freshly-grated nutmeg
Salt and fresh-milled black pepper
Chopped parsley to decorate

Pre-heat oven to gas mark 3, 325°F (170°C).

First heat half the dripping in a wide pan and brown the cutlets. Remove them from the pan and arrange them in a casserole with the sliced mushrooms (these don't need pre-cooking). Then add the rest of the dripping to the pan and leave aside.

To make the sauce, combine the redcurrant jelly, Worcestershire sauce and lemon juice in a saucepan (preferably non-stick) and stir continuously over a low heat until the ingredients are well and truly combined. Now heat the rest of the dripping in the frying-pan, add the flour and stir until it is golden brown. Then stir in the jelly mixture and sufficient red wine to make a thick gravy.

Stir and bring the mixture up to simmering point, season to taste with nutmeg, salt and freshly-milled black pepper and then pour the sauce over the cutlets, put a lid on and place the casserole in the oven and cook for 30 minutes. Then sprinkle on the chopped parsley and serve with new potatoes cooked in their skins and tossed in butter and freshly-chopped mint.

Moroccan Lamb Tagine

Recipe sent by
Miss M Durrant
Cardington
Bedfordshire

Serves 4 people

This is a typical North African dish, where meat and fruit are simmered together. We think this one is a real discovery, as new ideas for casseroles are hard to come by.

1½ lb (700 g) boned shoulder of lamb (weight after boning)
1½ tablespoons seasoned flour
3 tablespoons oil
2 medium onions (sliced)
2 green peppers (de-seeded and sliced)
1 small head of fennel
¾ pint (425 ml) vegetable stock
1 heaped teaspoon grated root ginger or
½ teaspoon ground ginger
2 generous pinches of saffron
1 strip of orange peel
4 oz (110 g) dried apricots (chopped)
1½ tablespoons lemon juice
Salt and freshly-milled black pepper

You will need a 4 to 5 pint (2½ litre) flameproof casserole. Pre-heat oven to gas mark 2, 300°F (150°C).

Start off by cutting the lamb into bite-sized cubes, removing any excess fat. Then coat the cubes in seasoned flour. Now heat 2 tablespoons of oil in a large frying-pan and fry the cubes of meat to seal and brown them nicely. So as not to overcrowd the pan and produce too much steam cook the meat in about 4 batches. As the pieces brown transfer them to the casserole. When all the meat is taken care of add another tablespoon of oil and cook the onions and pepper, just to brown them a little at the edges, too.

Remove any green fronds from the fennel and reserve them. Cut off the top, trim the root and cut the fennel in half and then in quarters. Transfer the peppers and onion to the meat and finally brown the fennel a little on all sides and transfer that too to the casserole. Next add the ginger, orange peel, the stock, and some seasoning and bring everything to simmering point.

Finally, crush the saffron to a powder with a pestle and mortar, ladle a little of the hot liquid on to it and let it soak for 5 minutes and then pour it in with the rest. Stir and put a lid on and cook in the oven for 1¾ hour. After that, add the apricots and lemon juice, replace the lid and cook for a further 15 minutes. This is very good served with brown rice.

Overleaf, left to right: Moroccan Lamb Tagine; Beef in Guinness with Orange Sauce page 60; Lamb Cutlets Shrewsbury page 69.

Pork Tenderloin with Cream and Cheese

Recipe sent by Carmen James-Agosti Leighton Buzzard Bedfordshire

Serves 4 people

This is a very simple but very rich and special dish which Carmen remembers comes from her Swiss grandmother and which was served at very special family occasions in Switzerland. We followed her recommendation and served this with fresh boiled noodles and a crisp green salad.

1½ lb (700 g) tenderloin of pork (cut into 1 inch or 2.5 cm thick medallions)
2 medium onions (finely chopped)
4 oz (110 g) grated Parmesan cheese (or a mixture of Parmesan and Cheddar)
½ pint (275 ml) double cream
A little butter
Salt and freshly-milled black pepper

Pre-heat oven to gas mark 6, 400°F (200°C).

First lightly butter a deep 3 pint (1.7 litre) ovenproof dish. Then arrange layers of meat (seasoned with salt and pepper), onions and finely grated cheese. You should get 2 layers: meat, onion, cheese, meat, onion, cheese.

Bake this in the oven for 50 minutes, then add the double cream and bake for a further 15 minutes, until golden brown. Serve with noodles and a fresh green salad.

Afelia (Marinated Pork with Coriander)

Recipe sent by Loulla Paul Edinburgh

Serves 4 people

This lovely Greek Cypriot recipe is best started off the night before so that the pork is marinated for a good length of time. It's a wonderful recipe for people at work who need something really good and fast for when they get home.

1½ lb (700 g) pork fillet
2 tablespoons coriander seeds
¼ pint (150 ml) dry red wine
2 tablespoons oil
2 fl. oz (55 ml) water
Salt and freshly-milled black pepper

The night before, trim any fat from the pork fillet and cut it into bite sized cubes, then put the cubes into a bowl. Using a pestle and mortar (or a bowl and the end of a rolling-pin), lightly crush the coriander seeds then sprinkle them all over the pork cubes and mix well. Now pour over the wine and stir everything again. Cover the bowl with a cloth and leave to marinate in the bottom of the fridge overnight.

Next day strain the pork in a large sieve over a bowl and reserve the marinade. Then heat the oil in a medium sized frying-pan; when it is really hot fry the pork pieces in 2 batches to brown them, removing the first batch to a plate, then returning them to the second batch. Then add the reserved marinade, bring to the boil, season and cover the pan with a lid and turn the heat down to a gentle simmer.

After 10 minutes, add the water and then re-cover the pan and cook gently for a further 30 minutes. Serve the afelia on a bed of rice. It is very nice accompanied by a Greek salad of tomatoes, onions, cucumber, olives and Feta cheese.

Chinese Red Roast Pork

Recipe sent by Elizabeth Bennett Croydon Surrey

Serves 4 people

This is delightful served either hot or cold – hot it would be good with the *South Sea Noodles* on page 39, or cold with the *Chinese Green Vegetable Salad* on page 122. It tastes better if you can leave it to marinate overnight.

1 lb (450 g) pork fillet (preferably in one piece)
1 tablespoon hoi sin sauce
1 tablespoon soy sauce
2 level teaspoons soft brown sugar
1 level teaspoon five spice powder
1 clove garlic (crushed)
1 teaspoon finely grated fresh ginger
Goundnut oil

Pre-heat oven to gas mark 7, 425 °F (220 °C).

The day before (or at least a couple of hours before) you need it, trim any fat from the pork but leave the fillet whole. Then in a small bowl mix together the hoi sin sauce, soy sauce, sugar, five spice powder, garlic and ginger. Place the meat in a shallow dish, rub or brush lightly with a little oil and then coat it with the sauce. The best way to do this is to use your hands, turning the meat over so that you get a complete coating. Now leave it to marinate and soak up all the flavours.

Place the pork on a rack in a roasting tin and spoon over any marinade, then brush lightly with a little more oil and roast in the oven for 10 minutes. Then reduce the heat to gas mark 4, 350°F (180°C) and cook for a further 30 minutes. Serve carved into thin slices.

Pork Vindaloo

Recipe sent by
Arati Ghose
Swansea
Wales

Serves 3 – 4 people

This is pork cooked in vinegar and roasting spices. If you don't like things too hot you can omit one of the chillies. It has a superb flavour and the aroma of roasted spices is most tantalising.

1 lb (450 g) lean pork shoulder (cut into bite-sized cubes)
½ pint (275 ml) water
1 teaspoon salt
1 heaped teaspoon cumin seeds
1 heaped teaspoon coriander seeds
2 inch (5 cm) stick cinnamon
4 – 6 black peppercorns
3 – 4 cloves
2 green cardamoms
2 small dried red chillies
1 inch (2.5 cm) piece of fresh ginger (grated)
2 – 3 cloves garlic (crushed)
3 tablespoons white wine vinegar
3 tablespoons groundnut oil
2 medium sized onions (sliced)
Salt and freshly-milled black pepper

First of all put the pork in a saucepan with the water and salt, then bring to the boil, cover and cook gently for about 30 minutes or until the pork is just tender. Skim the froth and remove from the heat.

Meanwhile, heat a thick, heavy frying-pan and add to it the cumin seeds, coriander seeds, the cinnamon, peppercorns, cloves, cardamoms and dried red chillies. Hold the pan above the flame and shake it constantly until the spices pop and start to smoke. Then cool them and after that blend them in a blender with the ginger and garlic and vinegar to make a paste, or crush to a paste in a pestle and mortar.

Next, in a medium frying-pan heat the oil and then fry the onions for about 10 minutes or until golden. Then pour in the processed spices and vinegar, fry for 2 – 3 minutes and then pour in the meat and liquid. Simmer until the meat is tender and the liquid has reduced to a sauce consistency, about 30 minutes. Finally taste and season. Serve with spiced rice (page 190) and chutney.

POULTRY AND GAME

Poulet Basque

Recipe sent anonymously

Serves 4 people

This recipe comes from a native of the Pyrénées, and she describes it as 'having all the flavours and colours typical of the South of France'.

1 fresh chicken (with giblets) weighing about 3½ lb (1.5 kg), cut into 8 pieces
8 oz (225 g) pork belly (cut into small chunks)
1 oz (25 g) butter
2 tablespoons olive oil
2 lb (900 g) fresh ripe tomatoes (skinned and quartered)
2 large green peppers (de-seeded and cut into strips)
8 oz (225 g) button mushrooms (halved)
¼ pint (150 ml) chicken stock (made with giblets)
1 clove garlic (crushed)
1 level teaspoon thyme (fresh or dried)
Salt and freshly-milled black pepper

Pre-heat oven to gas mark 6, 400°F (200°C).

Heat the butter and the oil together in a large flameproof casserole. When it is hot sauté the pieces of chicken and pork together until they are golden. Do this in 2 batches if there isn't enough room. Pour off the excess fat, then return the first batch to the casserole and add the stock, garlic, thyme, salt and freshly-milled black pepper to taste. Bring everything to simmering point, then transfer the casserole to the oven, cover with a lid, and cook for 30 minutes.

After 30 minutes add the tomatoes, peppers and mushrooms to the casserole and cook for a further 40 minutes, reducing the heat to gas mark 4, 350°F (180°C). This is good served with rice and a plain lettuce salad with a garlicky French dressing.

Chicken Parmigiana

Recipe sent by Margaret Wilson Kirkam Lancashire

Serves 4 people

This has a distinctly Italian Mediterranean taste. We like it served with brown rice and a lettuce salad.

4 chicken breasts (skinned and boned)
2 oz (50 g) freshly grated Parmesan cheese
2 oz (50 g) seasoned wholewheat flour
1 egg (beaten)
1 oz (25 g) butter
4 oz (110 g) Mozzarella cheese (sliced)
1 tablespoon olive oil
1 onion (chopped finely)
1 clove garlic (crushed)
2 – 3 courgettes (chopped small)
1 × 14 oz (400 g) Italian chopped tomatoes
1 tablespoon tomato purée
1 teaspoon each of dried basil and oregano
Salt and freshly-milled black pepper
Chopped parsley to garnish

Pre-heat oven to gas mark 4, 350 °F (180 °C).
You will need a casserole or baking dish at least 3 inches (7.5 cm) deep, or large enough to hold the chicken breasts in a single layer.

First of all mix the seasoned flour with 1 oz (25 g) of the Parmesan cheese. Then dip each chicken breast firstly in beaten egg and then in the flour and cheese mixture, coating each one on all sides.

Melt the butter in a frying-pan and when it is hot and foaming fry the chicken breasts until they are golden on all sides. Then transfer them to the baking dish and cover each portion with slices of Mozzarella cheese.

Now wipe the frying pan with kitchen paper and add the oil to it, and heat until it is.very hot. Soften the onion and garlic in it over a gentle heat for 5 minutes. Add the courgettes and cook these for 2 or 3 minutes, then add the tomatoes, tomato purée, basil, oregano and salt and freshly-milled black pepper. Let the sauce simmer gently for 20 minutes without covering.

After that pour the sauce over the chicken, cover loosely with foil and bake in the oven for 15 minutes. Then take off the foil and cook for a further 15 – 20 minutes. To serve, sprinkle the remaining Parmesan cheese and some fresh chopped parsley over.

Chicken in Spiced Peanut Butter Sauce

Serves 4 – 6 people

Recipe sent by
Mrs Ramsden
Runcorn
Cheshire

This recipe is on the same lines as the *West African Groundnut Stew* on page 63, only this one is with chicken and it rated very highly in the FOOD AID test kitchens!

One 4 lb (1.8 kg) chicken (with giblets) cut into 6 pieces
2 – 3 tablespoons groundnut oil
1 medium onion (chopped)
1 clove garlic (crushed)
1 green pepper (chopped)
8 oz (225 g) peanut butter
1 pint (570 ml) chicken stock (made with the giblets)
1 teaspoon turmeric
1 tablespoon ground coriander
1 teaspoon ground cumin
¼ teaspoon hot chilli powder
Salt and freshly-milled black pepper

First of all you heat 2 tablespoons of oil in a large flameproof casserole. Add the onion, garlic and green pepper and fry these gently until the onion is soft but not brown, about 10 minutes. Then remove the vegetables to a plate, turn up the heat and add a little more oil. As soon as it is hot add the chicken pieces and brown them on all sides, return the vegetables to the pan and remove it from the heat.

Now mix together the peanut butter, 4 fl. oz (110 ml) of the stock, the turmeric, coriander, cumin, chilli powder, and the salt and freshly-milled black pepper. Now stir this mixture into the saucepan containing the chicken and simmer and stir for 5 minutes.

Then stir in the remaining stock, cover and simmer on top of the stove for a further 30 minutes. After that uncover the casserole and cook for another 15 minutes or until the chicken is tender. Now taste to check the seasoning and serve. We like this served with brown rice or ribbon noodles.

Left: Orange Glazed Chicken with Coriander page 85. Right: Poulet Basque page 80.

Butter-Baked Spiced Chicken

Serves 3 – 4 people

Recipe sent anonymously

This is good served with lots of watercress and some lemon wedges to squeeze over, with the buttery juices served separately in a jug.

3 lb (1.35 kg) chicken
1 large clove of garlic
½ teaspoon salt
2 teaspoons green pepper berries
½ teaspoon ground cinnamon
½ teaspoon ground cumin
½ teaspoon ground coriander
2 oz (50 g) butter (at room temperature)
2 bayleaves

To serve
Lemon wedges and watercress

Pre-heat oven to gas mark 5, 375 °F (190 °C).

Begin by crushing the garlic together with the salt in a pestle and mortar, then add the green pepper berries and crush them as well. After that work in the cinnamon, cumin, coriander and softened butter. All this may be prepared in advance, but you'll need to bring it back to room temperature before using.

About an hour before you're ready to cook the chicken, loosen the skin on the breast of the chicken and gently release as far as the legs. Rub some of the spiced butter into the space between the skin and the flesh, then prick the thick part of the legs with a skewer (to allow the butter to penetrate) and rub some more butter into the skin all over the chicken, reserving a bit to place in the cavity along with the bayleaves. Sprinkle a little salt into the cavity as well.

Now leave the chicken for an hour at room temperature for the flavours to develop before cooking. Place the chicken on its side in a small shallow roasting dish and cook on the centre shelf for 1 hour (allowing 20 minutes) on each side and 20 minutes with the breast up), or until the chicken is cooked. Baste well each time the chicken is turned.

Orange-Glazed Chicken with Coriander

Recipe sent by
Bill Heath
Birmingham

Serves 4 people

This one is unbelievable at first sight but if you think about it, the pungent, burnt-orange flavour of coriander and the bitter-sweet, tangy flavour of Seville orange marmalade go wonderfully well with baked chicken.

4 chicken joints (quarters)
2 heaped teaspoons whole coriander seeds
4 tablespoons coarse cut Seville orange marmalade
2 cloves garlic (crushed)
1 teaspoon lemon juice
Salt and freshly-milled black pepper

Pre-heat oven to gas mark 5, 375 °F (190 °C).

First crush the coriander seeds finely in a pestle and mortar, then mix them with the marmalade, garlic and lemon juice.

Skin the chicken joints and place them in a roasting tin. Then make several cuts in the flesh, using a sharp knife, and rub salt and freshly-milled black pepper into them. Next spread the marmalade mixture all over the chicken joints and into the cuts and bake the chicken on a high shelf for about 40–45 minutes. Serve with jacket potatoes and a green salad.

Chicken Dragemiroff

Recipe sent by
Mary Gallagher
Liphook
Hampshire

Serves 2 people

This is a good recipe for using up left-over chicken. It is a Russian recipe given to Mary Gallagher by a Spanish waiter!

¾ – 1 lb (350 g – 450 g) left-over cooked chicken pieces (cut small)
1 medium onion (chopped)
1 oz (25 g) butter
¼ lb (110 g) mushrooms (sliced)
4 medium sized gherkins (sliced)
2 teaspoons tarragon (fresh or dried)
2 teaspoons sugar
3 fl. oz (75 ml) chicken stock
2 tablespoons sherry
¼ pt (150 ml) soured cream
Salt and freshly-milled black pepper

In a large, heavy frying-pan fry the onion in the butter until transparent. Then add the chicken pieces and stir well. Next, add the mushrooms and gherkins, stir and cook for a further 5 minutes. Then add the tarragon, sugar and a good seasoning of salt and freshly-milled black pepper. Pour in the stock and finally the sherry.

Then let it bubble and simmer for a couple of minutes, turn the heat to very low and lastly stir in the soured cream – to just heat through without boiling. This can be served with brown rice and a mixed salad with a good vinaigrette dressing.

Creamy Spiced Chicken

Recipe sent by
Shehzad Husain
Chislehurst
Kent

Serves 4 people

Shehzad, who contributed this recipe, is an expert on Indian cookery. We hope you enjoy her lovely chicken dish with its subtle flavours as much as we did.

1¾ lb (800 g) raw boned chicken (*ie* 4 small chicken breasts), cut into largish chunks
3 oz (75 g) unsalted butter
2 medium onions (thinly sliced)
2 bayleaves
1 teaspoon salt
¼ teaspoon coarsely ground black pepper
½ teaspoon garam masala
½ teaspoon ground coriander
A pinch of ground turmeric
1 tablespoon Worcestershire sauce
3 oz (75 g) small mushrooms
6 fl. oz (175 ml) double cream

In a heavy-based saucepan or flameproof casserole melt the butter over a medium heat and add the sliced onion. Fry this until soft and golden brown – about 10 minutes – then add the bayleaves and stir-fry for a further 1 minute.

Now add the chicken pieces to the onions, lower the heat and continue to stir-fry for another 5 minutes. After that add all the spices and seasoning and Worcestershire sauce and continue to stir-fry for a further 7 – 10 minutes, making sure all the chicken pieces are well-coated. Then add the mushrooms and stir these in, then gradually add the cream, mixing all the ingredients well together.

Finally, put a lid on and simmer gently over a very low heat for about 7 – 10 minutes or until the chicken is cooked. Serve this with spiced rice (see page 190) and chutney.

Marinated Pheasant in Port

Recipe sent by
Claire Ward
Monmouth
Gwent

Serves 6 – 8 people

This is a good way to cook pheasant a little later on in the season when roasting is risky. The sauce is very good and Claire Ward recommends a bottle of claret to drink with this.

1 brace of pheasants (ask the game dealer to skin and joint them for you and ask for the giblets for some stock)

For the marinade
¾ pint (425 ml) ruby port
2 onions (sliced)
2 cloves of garlic (chopped)
2 bayleaves (crumbled)
6 juniper berries (crushed)
Salt and freshly-milled black pepper

To finish
2 oz (50 g) butter
1 lb (450 g) button mushrooms
2 egg yolks
¼ pint (150 ml) double cream
Chopped parsley

Start off the day before by placing the joints of pheasant in a deep bowl, sprinkle in the onion, chopped garlic, bayleaves, juniper berries and salt and freshly-milled black pepper between them. Then pour over the port, cover with a cloth and leave to marinate overnight.

Meanwhile, make up some stock with the giblets and measure ½ pint (275 ml) into a jug. When you are ready to cook the pheasants pre-heat the oven to gas mark 4, 350°F (180°C).

Make sure you dry the pheasant pieces thoroughly with kitchen paper. Then melt the butter in a frying-pan and brown the joints on all sides before transferring them to a large flameproof casserole. Then add the mushrooms to the casserole with the marinade and ½ pint (275 ml) of stock and bring everything up to a gentle simmering point, put a lid on and transfer to the oven for 1 to 1¼ hours.

After that remove the pheasant joints and mushrooms to a warm serving dish, using a draining spoon, to keep warm. Then strain the sauce through a sieve into a saucepan, boil it briskly to reduce it by about one-third, then lower the heat till the sauce is just below simmering point. Beat the egg yolks and cream together and beat these into the sauce, taste and check the seasoning and then serve the pheasant with the sauce poured over; sprinkle it with chopped parsley. This is good served with spiced red cabbage.

Jugged Hare with Forcemeat Balls

Recipe sent by Sarah Americanos Limassol, Cyprus

Serves 4–6 people

Sarah, who lives in Cyprus, says she dreams from afar of her mother's jugged hare – 'sensational' is her description. Now the rest of us can share it with her.

1 young hare (about 3–4 lb or 1.35–1.8 kg) jointed into eight, complete with liver, heart, kidneys and reserved blood
Seasoned flour
1 tablespoon oil
1 tablespoon butter
2 medium-sized onions (chopped)
8 oz (225 g) streaky bacon (diced)
1 large onion stuck with 10 cloves
1 tablespoon flour
1 dessertspoon brown sugar
2 pints (1.25 l) of stock (made with the rib-cage of the hare simmered for 30 minutes with a carrot, onion, bayleaf and seasoning)
Salt and freshly-milled black pepper
1 teaspoon mixed dried herbs
2 bayleaves
8 fl. oz (225 ml) red wine
1 tablespoon redcurrant jelly

Pre-heat oven to gas mark 2, 300°F (150°C).

Arrange with your butcher to hang a young hare for a week to 10 days and to joint it into eight, reserving the blood (there should be 1 – 2 tablespoons) and the liver, heart and kidneys.

Start off by tossing the joints of hare in seasoned flour, then heat the oil and butter in a large frying-pan and brown the joints all over. Transfer them to a large heavy casserole that has a tight-fitting lid. Next fry the onions and streaky bacon in the same pan for 10 minutes and add these to the joints.

Now, into the centre plunge a large onion stuck with cloves, then sprinkle about 1 tablespoon of flour into the juices remaining in the frying-pan, add 1 dessertspoon of brown sugar and mix these together over a moderate heat. Then gradually add the stock to the pan, stirring all the time. When it starts to bubble and thicken, pour it over the contents of the casserole. Season generously with salt and pepper, and add the herbs and bayleaves. Bring everything up to simmering point, then place in the oven to cook for about 3 hours.

Before serving, mix the red wine with the redcurrant jelly and the reserved blood. Heat gently (but do *not* boil) then stir this into the casserole. Serve garnished with forcemeat balls (see below) and lovely creamy mashed potato.

Forcemeat Balls

The liver, heart and kidneys of hare
Salted cold water
1 onion (finely chopped)
6 oz (175 g) fresh white breadcrumbs
3 oz (75 g) shredded suet
2 teaspoons dried thyme
2 tablespoons fresh chopped parsley
Grated zest of 1 lemon
Salt and freshly-milled black pepper
1 egg
Lard for frying

Place the rinsed offal of the hare in a small pan, cover with cold salted water and bring to the boil slowly, then drain well and mince (or coarsely chop) the meat into a bowl. Now fry the onion in a little lard until soft, then add it to the minced offal together with the breadcrumbs, suet, herbs, lemon zest and seasoning. Add the egg to bind the mixture then, with floured hands, form into about 12 walnut-sized balls. Brown them all over in lard then serve as a garnish to the hare.

VEGETARIAN

Sarah Brown's Florentine Loaf

Serves 4 people

Recipe sent by Sarah Brown

This recipe has been kindly supplied by Sarah Brown, the doyenne of vegetarian cooking in Britain, who has been a great support to FOOD AID.

4 oz (110 g) red lentils (washed)
8 fl. oz (225 ml) water
1 onion (peeled and finely chopped)
1 tablespoon sunflower oil
1 teaspoon garam masala
1 clove garlic (crushed)
12 oz (350 g) spinach (washed and finely shredded)
4 oz (110g) cottage cheese
1 large egg
Juice of ½ a lemon
2 tablespoons finely chopped coriander leaves
Salt and freshly-milled black pepper
Nutmeg

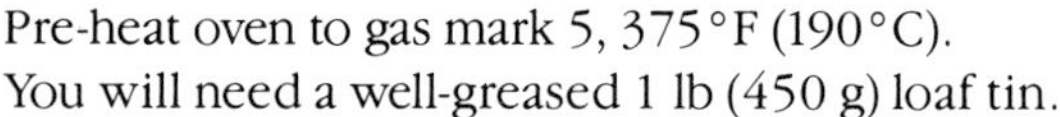

Pre-heat oven to gas mark 5, 375 °F (190 °C).
You will need a well-greased 1 lb (450 g) loaf tin.

Cook the lentils with the water in a tightly covered pan for about 15 – 20 minutes. Then beat to a smooth purée with a wooden spoon, adding a little more water and cooking for longer if necessary.

Cool the mixture and meanwhile fry the onion in the oil for 5 – 6 minutes. Add the garam masala and garlic and cook for a further 2 minutes. Now add the finely shredded spinach to the pan, cover and cook for a further 5 – 6 minutes or until the spinach has collapsed and is fairly well cooked.

Purée this mixture for 30 seconds in a food processor or blender. Then blend this mixture with the cooked lentils, cottage cheese, egg, lemon juice and coriander leaves. Season well with salt, freshly-milled black pepper and nutmeg. Now spoon the mixture into the prepared tin and bake for 45 – 50 minutes. Allow the loaf to cool in the tin for 10 minutes before turning it out. Serve hot, cut in slices with a fresh tomato sauce (see page 187).

Bulgar Wheat with Mushrooms

Serves 4 people as a main course or 8 as an accompaniment

Recipe sent by
Chloe Voyias
Ilford
Essex

For a vegetarian this could be a complete supper dish but for non-vegetarians it would be a nice accompaniment to spicy sausages or something grilled.

8 oz (225 g) bulgar wheat
5 tablespoons oil
1 medium onion (skinned and chopped)
½ green pepper (de-seeded and chopped)
2 ripe tomatoes (skinned and finely chopped)
½ green apple (cored, diced and skin left on)
½ pint (275 ml) vegetable stock (see page 187)
Salt and freshly-milled black pepper

For the mushroom mixture
8 oz (225 g) mushrooms (wiped and sliced)
¼ pint (150 ml) red wine
2 tablespoons coriander seeds (lightly crushed)
Parsley to garnish

First heat the oil in a saucepan over a medium heat, then add the chopped onion and pepper and fry until golden brown, stirring from time to time, for about 8 minutes. Then add the tomatoes and continue to fry for a further 2 minutes, turning the mixture well.

Lower the heat to its lowest setting and add the bulgar wheat, then stir with a wooden spoon for 5 minutes, turning the mixture over well to make sure the bulgar is well coated with the oil mixture. Then stir in the apple and pour in the stock (still on the lowest heat). Now stir again until all the stock has been absorbed, taste, and season well. Switch off the heat, cover the saucepan and leave it to stand for 10 minutes.

Meanwhile, put the mushrooms, wine, coriander and some seasoning into another small saucepan and simmer them together for 10 minutes, by which time the mushrooms will have turned a lovely pinky colour.

To serve, press the bulgar mixture into a 2 ½ pint (1.5 litre) ring mould, then turn it out on to a warm serving dish. Spoon the mushroom mixture into the centre, and garnish with parsley.

Hazelnut and Mushroom Roast

Serves 4–6 people

Recipe sent by
Wilf Wilson
Esh Winning
Durham

Our FOOD AID tester, Heather, said she could convert to being a vegetarian after tasting this, and we all agree – excellent!

Long grain brown rice (measured to the 5 fl. oz or 150 ml level in a glass measuring jug)
10 fl. oz (275 ml) boiling water
1 teaspoon salt
A little vegetable oil
½ level teaspoon celery seeds
1 large onion (peeled and chopped)
4 oz (110 g) mushrooms (wiped and chopped)
2 medium carrots (pared and grated)
1 tablespoon soy sauce
4 oz (110 g) wholemeal breadcrumbs
6 oz (175 g) ground hazelnuts
½ level teaspoon dried sage
1 teaspoon yeast extract
Sunflower seeds

Pre-heat oven to gas mark 4, 350°F (180°C).
You will need a 2 lb (900 g) loaf tin.

Cook the rice first by heating 1 dessertspoon of oil in a small saucepan and stirring in the rice to give it a light coating of oil. Now measure 10 fl. oz (275 ml) of boiling water from the kettle, add this to the rice along with 1 level teaspoon of salt. Stir once, put on a lid and let the rice cook for approximately 40 minutes or until all the liquid has been absorbed.

Meanwhile heat 1 tablespoon of oil in a medium-sized frying-pan and add the celery seeds, onion, mushrooms, carrots and soy sauce. Mix them together and let them cook gently for about 10 minutes.

Then in a large bowl combine the cooked brown rice, breadcrumbs, hazelnuts, sage and the vegetable mixture and mix everything thoroughly together. Now dissolve the yeast extract in 3 fl. oz (75 ml) hot water and stir this into the rest of the ingredients.

Place the mixture into the loaf tin, sprinkle the surface with sunflower seeds and bake in the oven for 45 minutes.

Then leave it to cool in the tin for 5 minutes before turning it out. Serve sliced (though it will be rather crumbly), accompanied perhaps by crunchy roast potatoes, steamed vegetables and a homemade tomato sauce (see page 187). It's also very good cold with any of the FOOD AID chutneys and a crisp salad.

Gillygate Bean Casserole

Recipe sent by Gillygate Wholefood Bakery Gillygate York

Serves 6 people

This is a highly nutritious bean casserole and amazingly economical – I like to serve it topped with a crusty cheese, herb and breadcrumb topping.

8 oz (225 g) haricot beans
8 oz (225 g) black-eyed beans
(both soaked in lots of cold water overnight or for at least 12 hours)
1 teaspoon brown sugar
2 teaspoons chutney
1 large onion (chopped)
2 oz (50 g) butter or margarine
2 oz (50 g) wholemeal flour
½ pint (275 ml) milk
¼ teaspoon dried ginger
¼ teaspoon dried mustard
1 level teaspoon each of oregano, thyme, sweet basil
Salt and freshly-milled black pepper

For the topping
2 oz (50 g) grated Cheddar cheese with chives
1 tablespoon freshly chopped parsley
1 heaped tablespoon wholewheat breadcrumbs

First of all, cook the beans by straining them in a colander, then covering them with plenty of cold water. Bring them to the boil and simmer for 40 minutes or until the beans are tender, then strain them in the colander again and return to the pan.

Pre-heat oven to gas mark 4, 350°F (180°C).

Make up the sauce by first melting the butter in a saucepan, then gently sweat the onion for about 6 minutes or until soft. Now stir in the flour, mustard, and ginger and then gradually stir in the milk, a little at a time until you have a smooth sauce. Season with salt and freshly-milled black pepper and at this stage add the herbs.

Pour the sauce over the beans, mix well and transfer to a 3 pint (1.75 litre) baking dish or casserole, then stir in the sauce plus the brown sugar and 2 teaspoons of chutney, and mix everything thoroughly.

Finally, mix the cheese, parsley and breadcrumbs together and sprinkle these all over the surface of the beans and bake the whole thing in the oven for about 35 to 40 minutes or until the top is brown and bubbling. This is good served with a tomato and onion salad in a sharp lemon dressing.

A Gratin of Mushrooms and Green Beans

Serves 6 people

Recipe sent by Margaret Taylor Kendal Cumbria

We used the tiny haricot vert beans for this, but feel it would also work very well with sliced runner beans. Either way, it's extremely good.

1½ oz (40 g) butter or margarine
1 large onion (finely chopped)
¼ lb (110 g) mushrooms (sliced)
1 lb (450 g) haricots verts (topped and tailed, cut into 1½ inch or 4 cm lengths)
3 fl. oz (75 ml) soured cream
4 oz (110 g) Mozzarella cheese (grated)
½ teaspoon fresh thyme (or ¼ teaspoon dried)
½ teaspoon salt
Freshly-milled black pepper

Pre-heat oven to gas mark 7, 425°F (220°C).

First heat the butter or margarine in a largish saucepan, then add the chopped onion and cook over a low to medium heat until softened but not coloured – about 5 minutes.

Now add the sliced mushrooms to the onion, stir and

continue to cook for 3 minutes before adding the prepared beans, the thyme, salt and some freshly-milled pepper. Turn the heat down to very low, put a lid on the pan and cook the mushrooms and beans in their own juices for 5 minutes, stirring them from time to time.

Next spread half of them in a buttered gratin dish, pour in the soured cream, spreading it evenly over them, then arrange the rest of the bean and mushroom mixture over that. Finally sprinkle the Mozzarella cheese over the surface and bake in the oven for 15 minutes. Serve hot.

Mexican Bean Pie

Recipe sent by
Rosemary Grant
Brussels
Belgium

Serves 2 people as a snack or 1 as a main course

This has an unusual oatmeal batter, filled with cheese and a Mexican bean mixture. The best cheese, we think, is a very strong, sharp, matured Cheddar.

For the batter
2 oz (50 g) porridge oats
¼ pint (150 ml) water (cold)
½ oz (10 g) bran
1 oz (25 g) plain flour
1 egg
1½ tablespoons sugar
½ tablespoon baking powder
1 tablespoon oil
1 tablespoon milk
1 teaspoon lemon juice

For the filling
5 oz (150 g) matured Cheddar cheese (grated)
1 small tin of kidney beans (drained and rinsed)
1 medium onion (chopped)
1 clove garlic (crushed)
1 small green pepper (chopped)
Salt and freshly-milled black pepper
1½ tablespoons oil
2 good pinches cayenne pepper

Pre-heat the oven to gas mark 4, 350°F (180°C).
For this you will need a 2 pint (1.25 litre) buttered soufflé or baking dish.

Begin by soaking the oats in the water in a mixing bowl for about 5 minutes to soften. Then add all the other batter ingredients to the oats and water and give the whole lot a really good mixing, either with a large fork or a whisk.

Next, heat the oil in a frying pan and soften both the onion and green pepper in it for 5 minutes, then add the garlic and cook for another 5 minutes. To this add the beans, the seasoning and a couple of good pinches of cayenne pepper, or more if you like a really Mexican zing!

Pour half of the batter into the baking dish, sprinkle half of the cheese over and then add the bean mixture, followed by the rest of the cheese and the remainder of the batter. Then bake in the oven for 30 to 40 minutes. We like to serve this with a crunchy, well-dressed salad.

Hot Green Banana Curry

Serves 3 – 4 people

Recipe sent by Angela Moules Salisbury Wiltshire

If you want a milder version of this you could of course cut the chilli content. It is good served with spiced pilau rice and a tomato and onion salad dressed in lemon juice. Green bananas are obtainable in most West Indian shops.

8 green bananas
2 tablespoons oil
1 large onion (finely chopped)
1 inch (2.5 cm) fresh ginger (peeled and finely chopped)
1 teaspoon tumeric
1 level teaspoon chilli powder
The seeds of 4 green cardamoms (crushed in a pestle and mortar)
1 – 2 fresh green chillies
8 fl. oz (225 ml) water
8 fl. oz (225 ml) plain yoghurt
1 teaspoon garam masala

First, heat the oil in a large saucepan and fry the onion with the ginger for about 8 minutes, until it is softened and golden. Then add the tumeric and chilli powder, cardamoms and fresh chillies and cook everything for about 1 minute.

Next, peel the bananas – you need to do this with a small sharp knife as they do not peel like ripe bananas at all; the skin needs to be removed rather like peeling a cucumber. Cut the bananas across into slices, about ⅓ inch (8 mm) thick. Then stir them into the onion and spice mixture and allow them to brown slightly.

Now add 8 fl. oz (225 ml) water, stir everything and then cover and cook gently until soft, about 10 – 15 minutes. Finally, stir in the yoghurt and garam masala and continue to cook gently for a further 2 minutes. (Add a little additional water if you think that it needs it.) Lastly, taste, season and serve hot.

Anna Wing's Cheddar Cheese and Vegetable Roast

Serves 3 – 4 people

Recipe sent by Anna Wing

This is gorgeous – so much so that if there's any left you are likely to take a little mouthful each time you open the fridge. Which is a good reason for making enough to serve cold the next day!

1 small green pepper (chopped small)
1 small red pepper (chopped small)
1 medium onion (chopped small)
12 oz (350 g) fresh mushrooms (chopped)
3 celery sticks (chopped small)
8 oz (225 g) wholewheat breadcrumbs
6 oz (175 g) mature Cheddar cheese (or similar) grated
1 large egg
3 tablespoons oil
Salt and freshly-milled black pepper

Pre-heat oven to gas mark 5, 375 °F (190 °C).
You will need a 2 pint (1.25 litre) ovenproof dish, lightly greased.

Heat the oil in a large saucepan or frying-pan and cook the peppers and onion for 5 minutes. Then add the mushrooms and celery and continue to cook till all the vegetables are tender, keeping the heat fairly low. In all it will take about 10 – 12 minutes. Then remove the pan from the heat and stir in 6 oz (175 g) of the breadcrumbs and 4 oz (110 g) of the cheese. Beat the egg with some salt and freshly-milled black pepper and add that to the pan, stirring and mixing everything thoroughly together.

Spoon the mixture into the baking dish and level the surface with the back of a spoon. Now mix the remaining cheese and breadcrumbs together and sprinkle this mixture over the top.

Place the dish in the oven and bake for 25 minutes or until the top is golden brown. Serve hot or cold – either way it is good with a salad.

Brother Joseph's Spaghetti for One

Recipe sent by Brother Joseph Liss Hants

Serves 1 person

In this delightful supper dish for one Brother Joseph has managed to create a meeting point between Italian and Chinese cooking and the results are highly recommended.

2 oz (50 g) spaghetti (broken up a little)
1 teacupful finely shredded white cabbage
1 egg
1 small clove garlic (finely minced)
1 dessertspoon dark soy sauce
1 teaspoon vinegar
1 heaped dessertspoon butter (approx. 1 – 1½ oz or 40 g) divided into 4 equal portions
Salt and pepper to taste

Put the spaghetti into boiling water and boil until tender. Drain and stir in the first portion of butter to keep the strands separate. While the spaghetti is boiling, use a large roomy frying-pan to fry the cabbage in the second portion of butter for about 4 minutes until it has softened a little.

Now push the cabbage to the side of the pan away from direct heat, then fry the garlic in the third portion of butter for a couple of minutes. Add the spaghetti and soy sauce and stir-fry everything, including the cabbage. When heated through, push everything to the side of the pan. Melt the last portion of butter and fry the egg, mushing it with the vinegar.

Before the egg gets hard, but *not* while it is still runny, mix everything together. Add salt and pepper to taste and serve at once on a heated plate.

To vary this dish it could be garnished liberally with grated cheese, chopped ham or flaked cooked smoked haddock.

Wholewheat Vegetable Lasagne

Recipe sent by Brenda Bordon

Serves 4 people

No need to miss out on baked lasagne if you don't eat meat – vegetarians have thought up lots of variations and this is a very good one.

6 oz (175 g) wholewheat lasagne
1 large onion (chopped)
4 oz (110 g) green pepper (chopped)
8 oz (225 g) courgettes (washed and chopped)
4 oz (110 g) mushrooms (sliced)
14 oz (400 g) tin of Italian chopped tomatoes
1 tablespoon tomato purée
6 fl. oz (175 ml) red wine
1 teaspoon basil
1 teaspoon oregano
1½ tablespoons of olive oil (for frying)
1 clove of garlic (crushed)
Salt and freshly-milled black pepper

For the sauce
1 oz (25 g) wholemeal flour
1 oz (25 g) butter
12 fl. oz (350 ml) milk
Freshly grated nutmeg
4 oz (110 g) cheese (grated)
Parmesan cheese to sprinkle over the top

Pre-heat oven to gas mark 5, 375°F (190°C).
You will need a 3 pint (1.75 litre) oblong heatproof dish.

Begin by cooking the lasagne according to the instructions on the packet. I find it best to cook the lasagne 3 squares at a time for about 5 minutes or until they float to the surface and slip them into a bowl of cold water to prevent them clogging together. When all the pasta is cooked, drain in a colander and prepare the vegetable filling.

First, heat the oil in a frying-pan and add the onion and pepper and cook these over a medium heat until they are soft, about 5 minutes. Then add the courgettes, mushrooms and garlic and continue to cook for a further 5 minutes, stirring every now and then to prevent it browning too much. Now add the tomatoes, tomato purée, wine and herbs, and a good seasoning of salt and freshly-milled black pepper. Turn the heat down to low and simmer this mixture gently for about 10 minutes.

Meanwhile, make up the sauce by placing the flour, butter and milk together in a saucepan. Whisk these together over a medium to low heat until they are thoroughly blended and then when the sauce has come to the boil and thickened, season it with salt, freshly-milled black pepper and a good grating of whole nutmeg. Now stir in the cheese until it has melted and remove the sauce from the heat.

To assemble the lasagne, put first a layer of vegetable mixture over the base of the dish, follow it with a layer of lasagne, then repeat this and finish off by pouring the cheese sauce all over as the final layer. Now sprinkle the top with the Parmesan cheese and bake in the oven for 35–40 minutes, or until the surface is golden brown and crusty. Serve with a crisp green salad with a sharp lemony dressing.

Casserole of Winter Vegetables

Serves 6–8 people

Recipe sent by
Jenny Mathers
Riding Mill
Northumberland

Although this comes in the vegetarian section it's so good I'm sure most meat-eaters would be entirely satisfied with it and not notice the absence of meat.

8 oz (225 g) red kidney beans (dried weight)
2 tablespoons oil
1 large onion (finely chopped)
4 sticks celery (finely chopped)

2 small turnips or ½ large swede (chopped into dice)
3 small parsnips (chopped into dice)
2 large carrots (chopped into dice)
4 oz (110 g) mushrooms
½ tablespoon wholewheat flour
½ tablespoon wheatgerm
1 teaspoon yeast extract
2 teaspoons peanut butter
1 large tin Italian tomatoes (14 oz or 400 g)
1 bayleaf
2 tablespoons fresh parsley
1 teaspoon dried marjoram
½ teaspoon dried rosemary
½ teaspoon dried sage

Pre-heat oven to gas mark 6, 400°F (200°C).

Cover the kidney beans with boiling water to give 1 inch (2.5 cm) extra water over them, then leave them to soak for an hour at least. After that rinse the beans in fresh water and place in a large saucepan with water to cover the beans by 1 inch (2.5 cm), then simmer with a lid on for 45–60 minutes or until the beans are tender (ensure the beans are cooked at a rapid boil for a minimum of 12 minutes).

Meanwhile, heat the oil in a frying-pan and sauté the onion and celery for 5 minutes then add the diced root vegetables, turn them in the oil and then add the mushrooms, either as whole buttons or quartered if they are large. Now cook everything, with frequent stirring, for a further 5 minutes and then add the flour and wheatgerm. Stir well and then over a low heat add the stock (which you make by dissolving the yeast extract and peanut butter in ¾ pint (425 ml) boiling water), a little at a time, stirring constantly. Then, still stirring, bring the mixture up to simmering point and cook for 2–3 minutes.

Finally add the tinned tomatoes, herbs and the cooked and drained kidney beans. Pour everything into a 3½ pint (2 litre) casserole dish, cover and cook in the oven for 1–1½ hours. Serve with jacket or boiled potatoes and a lightly steamed green vegetable.

Overleaf, left: Spiced Almond Risotto page 107. Right: Gillygate Bean Casserole page 95.

Peter Langan's Potato and Onion Soufflés with Parsley Sauce

Serves 4 people

Recipe sent by Peter Langan

On a personal note here: when I was 22 and learning to cook, two people reigned supreme in the cookery world as far as I was concerned. One was Elizabeth David, whose books influenced me more than anyone else's, and the other was Peter Langan whose ideas and attitude to food have been constantly echoed by my own instincts and aspirations. Here is a typical example.

½ pint (275 ml) béchamel sauce (made with 1½ oz or 40 g of butter, 1 oz or 25 g flour, and ½ pint or 275 ml milk infused with a bayleaf, a few peppercorns, a pinch of mace, a garlic clove, and a little carrot and celery)
2 medium potatoes (approx. 10 – 11 oz or 275 – 300 g)
Salt (see recipe)
1 large onion (6 oz or 175 g) finely chopped
2 oz (50 g) butter
Salt and freshly-milled black pepper

For the parsley sauce
½ pint (275 ml) white sauce (made with 1 oz or 25 g butter, ¾ oz or 20 g flour and ½ pint or 275 ml milk)
1 tablespoon cream
1 oz (25 g) parsley stalks
2 tablespoons fresh chopped parsley leaves
Salt and freshly-milled black pepper

Pre-heat the oven to gas mark 6, 400°F (200°C).
You'll also need four 4½ inch (11.5 cm) ramekin dishes well-buttered and dusted with flour.

Cook the potatoes first: they should be washed and well dried, then placed on a ½ inch (1 cm) bed of cooking salt in a small gratin dish or similar. Bake on a high shelf in a hot oven for about an hour.

While that's cooking, make up the white sauce and add the parsley stalks to it, then leave it in a warm place to infuse the flavour of the parsley stalks. This would be a good moment to make up the béchamel sauce as well.

When the potatoes are cooked reduce the heat to gas mark 4, 350° (180°C). Using an oven glove to protect your hands, peel off the skins and use a spoon to push the warm potato through a sieve into a mixing bowl. You are going to need 8 oz of potato, so weigh that amount and return it to the bowl – the birds will love the leftovers!

Now for the soufflé. In a medium-sized saucepan heat 2 oz (50 g) of butter and cook the onion very gently over a low heat for about 12 minutes till softened but not browned. Now add the onion to the potato along with the béchamel sauce and the egg yolks, and mix all these together thoroughly, seasoning well.

Next, in a roomy grease-free bowl, whisk the egg whites till stiff and fold these gradually and carefully into the potato mixture. Place the ramekin dishes on a baking sheet and spoon the soufflé mixture into them. Then bake them for 15 to 20 minutes or until well-risen and golden-brown on top.

While the soufflés are cooking, sieve the parsley stalks out of the white sauce, then gently re-heat it adding a tablespoon of cream. Stir in the fresh chopped parsley at the last minute. Serve the soufflés with the sauce separately in a jug.

Spiced Almond Risotto

Recipe sent anonymously

Serves 4 people

This is a beautiful, colourful risotto – extra good if you lightly toast the almonds to make them crunchier. Serve this to carnivores and they won't miss the meat!

6 oz (175 g) long grain brown rice (uncooked weight)
4 oz (110 g) blanched almonds
4 oz (110 g) mushrooms (wiped and sliced)
1 red pepper (de-seeded and cut into strips)
3 sticks of celery (sliced diagonally)
1 onion (peeled and chopped)
3 tablespoons olive oil
1 clove of garlic (crushed)
1 teaspoon grated fresh root ginger
2 oz (50 g) sultanas
1 teaspoon cinnamon
1 teaspoon crushed coriander seeds
1 pint boiling water
Salt and freshly-milled black pepper

To garnish
Lemon wedges dipped in Paprika

For this you will need, ideally, a large frying-pan with a lid.

Begin by heating the oil in the pan, then soften the onion and pepper in it for 5 minutes. Next add the garlic and ginger and cook for a few seconds before adding the mushrooms, celery and sultanas. Stir these around and cook for a further 5 minutes; during that time add the spices.

Now stir in the rice, turning it around in the mixture to get it nicely coated with oil, then pour in 1 pint of boiling water. Add some salt, stir once, put the lid on the pan, then turn the heat to its lowest possible setting and let everything cook for 40 minutes – until the rice is tender and all the liquid has been absorbed.

Halfway through the cooking time sprinkle in the almonds and replace the lid. During the last 10 minutes of cooking check the risotto to make sure that it doesn't stick. As long as there is still some moisture left all should be well. Season to taste with salt and pepper and serve the risotto with lemon wedges that have had their edges dipped in paprika.

Potato Base Pizza

Serves 4 people

Recipe sent by
Margaret Kellett
Markfield
Leicestershire

This is a quick and easy pizza and the potato base makes an interesting change. This is also good served cold.

For the base
8 oz (225 g) boiled potatoes (skins may be left on for added fibre)
2 oz (50 g) margarine or butter
4 oz (110 g) self-raising flour
Salt and freshly-milled black pepper

For the topping
6 oz (175 g) mature Cheddar (thinly sliced)
8 oz (225 g) onions (thinly sliced)
1 red pepper (thinly sliced)
1 clove garlic (crushed)

2 tablespoons olive oil
4 oz (110 g) mushrooms (sliced)
2 teaspoons red wine vinegar
½ level tablespoon oregano
2 tablespoons tomato purée
Salt and freshly-milled black pepper

Pre-heat oven to gas mark 6, 400°F (200°C).
You will need an oiled baking tray.

First of all, boil the potatoes until they are soft and then mash them to pulp with the butter. Sift in the flour and add a little salt and freshly-milled black pepper. Now mix to a dough, transfer on to a floured surface and knead lightly until the mixture becomes soft and elastic. Then roll it out to a 10 inch (25.5 cm) round and place this on to the oiled baking sheet.

Next heat the olive oil in a large frying-pan and fry the onions, red pepper and garlic for 5 minutes. Then stir in the mushrooms, vinegar and oregano and a seasoning of salt and freshly-milled black pepper. Now spread the tomato purée all over the pizza base and then top with the onion and pepper mixture, and finally place the slices of cheese all over.

Bake the pizza on a high shelf in the oven for 40 minutes; have a look after 30 minutes and cover with foil if the top looks too brown. Serve hot or cold with a salad.

VEGETABLES AND SALADS

Artichoke Fritters

Serves 4–6 people

Recipe sent by
Octavia Hare
Luton
Bedfordshire

The flavour of caraway blends beautifully with Jerusalem artichokes in these little fritters. Try serving them with grilled meat instead of potatoes, or on their own in a tomato sauce.

8 oz (225 g) Jerusalem artichokes
2 oz (50 g) oats
1 oz (25 g) bran
2 oz (50 g) plain flour
1 small onion (finely chopped)
1 clove garlic (finely chopped)
1 teaspoon caraway seeds
A pinch of bicarbonate of soda
1 tablespoon oil
1 egg (beaten)
Salt and freshly-milled black pepper

For frying
¼ pint (150 ml) oil

Scrub and peel the artichokes and then grate them into a bowl and mix thoroughly with all the rest of the ingredients and the seasoning.

Then take small amounts of the mixture and roll into walnut-sized rounds (a little oil on the palms of your hands will help you here), and then flatten the rounds into discs, about 1½ – 2 inches (4–5 cm) in diameter.

Now heat the oil in a frying-pan over a medium heat and as soon as it is really hot, shallow fry the fritters for about 3 minutes on each side. Drain them on kitchen paper before serving.

Red Cabbage with Bacon and Walnuts

Serves 4–5 people

Recipe sent by
Catherine Calland
St. Briavels
Monmouthshire

Here is an excellent alternative way to cook red cabbage – particularly when you haven't got the time to bake it for hours in the oven. In this recipe it is sliced very finely then steamed and served with crispy bacon and walnuts.

1 small red cabbage (weighing 1 – 1¼ lb or 450 – 560 g)
5 rashers of smoked streaky bacon
1½ oz (40 g) walnut pieces (chopped)
1 oz (25 g) butter
Salt and freshly-milled black pepper

Before you start have ready a steamer set over a saucepan of simmering water. Prepare the cabbage by discarding any damaged outer leaves, slicing it into four, then cutting each quarter obliquely to remove the white core. Now slice the cabbage very finely (or you could do this with the shredder of a food processor), transfer it to the steamer and cover. Steam for 4 – 5 minutes, or until cooked, then drain thoroughly.

While that's happening, remove the bacon rind and cut each rasher into small strips. Heat ½ oz (10 g) of the butter in a medium frying-pan and fry the bacon until the fat runs and the bacon is crispy. Add the walnuts to the pan followed by the drained cabbage (which at this stage will look a sort of blue-purple but will regain its colour on contact with the bacon). Add the remaining ½ oz (10 g) of butter and heat briefly, stirring the contents of the pan. Taste and season with salt and pepper before serving.

Lemon Cooked Chicory

Serves 4 people

Recipe sent by
Heidi Lascelles
'Books for Cooks'
London

This is very good served with grilled chicken and possibly a new potato or two.

1½ lb (700 g) chicory (*ie* 4 good sized heads)
Zest and juice of 1 large lemon
1 tablespoon brandy
5 – 6 tablespoons olive oil
1 clove of garlic (crushed)
Salt and freshly-milled black pepper

Prepare the chicory heads by cutting them in half lengthways. Then using a sharp knife cut out an inverted 'v' from the core at the base of the heads.

Now heat ½ inch (1 cm) of boiling salted water in a pan which is large enough to take the chicory in a single layer.

When you have added them bring them back to the boil, cover and simmer gently for 8 – 10 minutes. Now drain them thoroughly in a colander and then return the chicory to the hot pan and add the rest of the ingredients. Cover the pan and heat for a few moments, just enough to allow the ingredients to heat through and permeate the chicory.

Corn on the Cob African Style

Recipe sent by
Mrs Shila Kotecha
Addiscombe
Surrey

Serves 4 people as a starter or 2 as a main course

Like all corn on the cob recipes this one definitely needs napkins tucked into collars and finger-bowls all round, as well as two forks per person. If you are prepared for a little manoeuvring, the results are delicious; alternatively, you could make up the sauce and then cook some frozen sweetcorn kernels in it instead.

4 corn on the cob (each cut across into 4 pieces)
2 tablespoons cooking oil
½ teaspoon each of whole cumin and mustard seeds
5 fl. oz (150 ml) natural yoghurt
1 lb fresh ripe tomatoes (skinned and chopped) or
a 14 oz (400 g) tin of Italian chopped tomatoes
A generous 4 oz (110 g) peanuts, coarsely ground
A scant 2 oz (50 g) desiccated coconut
1 – 2 green chillies (de-seeded and finely chopped)
½-inch (1 cm) piece of fresh root ginger (peeled and grated)
Salt

For this you need a large, deep saucepan.

Begin by heating the oil in the saucepan, then add the cumin and mustard seeds. When the heat begins to draw out their aroma and flavour, add the sweetcorn pieces, turning them around in the oil so that they are well coated. Add the tomatoes, ground peanuts, chillies and ginger.

Stir everything to mix evenly, then lower the heat and leave to simmer gently for 10 – 15 minutes, stirring a few times to make sure that each piece of sweetcorn is well coated with sauce. Add some salt and the coconut, have another good stir to mix it in, and continue to simmer for a further 5 minutes. Finally, stir in the yoghurt, mix well again, then serve at once.

Glynn Christian's Real Baked Beans

Serves 6–8 people

Recipe sent by Glynn Christian

Not just real baked beans – but smoked bacon, garlic sausage and tomatoes simmered with the beans to permeate them with lovely flavours and produce a rich, thick sauce.

1 lb (450 g) dried haricot or cannellini beans
1¾ – 2½ lb (800g – 1 kg) plum tomatoes (in their juice)
2 onions (sliced)
4 – 6 whole garlic cloves
3 bayleaves
12 oz (350 g) smoked bacon (cubed)
12 oz (350 g) garlic sausage (sliced)
1 small glass red wine (4 fl. oz or 110 ml)
Salt and freshly-milled black pepper

Soak the beans overnight and drain them in a colander. Then cook them in plenty of unsalted water until they are tender but not falling to pieces, about 30 minutes. Drain them and put into a large flameproof casserole that has a good tight-fitting lid together with all the remaining ingredients except the wine. Glynn says 'although these are called baked beans I always find it better to cook them on the top of the stove as this is easier and safer when checking their condition'.

Place the casserole over the gentlest possible heat and cook for at least 2 hours, by which time a lot of the fat will have melted and been absorbed, and some of the beans will have dissolved to form, with the tomatoes, a rich, thick sauce. Check every now and then and give everything a good stirring. Towards the end add the wine, and taste to check the seasoning.

Glynn also says it is even better next day but you will need to add more tomatoes and wine for reheating.

Overleaf, left to right: Corn on the Cob African Style page 114; Chinese Green Vegetable Salad page 122; Italian Potatoes and Sweet Peppers page 118.

Coconut Sambal

Recipe sent by
Tom Kemp
Haughly
Suffolk

Serves 6–8 people as an accompaniment

This recipe – originally from Sri Lanka – makes a wonderful accompaniment to almost any curry. It should be served chilled, which makes a nice contrast to the hot curry. It is meant to be quite spicy and a little of it goes a long way, but you can cut down on the chilli powder if you want it a bit more tame.

1 medium-sized onion
5 oz (150 g) finely grated fresh coconut
5 teaspoons lemon juice
1 level teaspoon paprika
½ teaspoon salt
½ teaspoon chilli powder

First, peel the onion, then grate it quite finely into a mixing bowl. Add the grated coconut and combine it well with the onion. Now add the rest of the ingredients and blend them in thoroughly – if you possess a liquidiser or food processor, that will do the job beautifully.

Cover the bowl with foil or clingfilm, then chill the sambol in the refrigerator until ready to serve. Transfer to a serving-bowl so that everyone can help themselves.

Italian Potatoes and Sweet Peppers

Recipe sent by
Linda Bond
Thorpe Bay
Essex

Serves 3 people

Linda's recipe is from an ancient Italian cook book and it's an unusual way of cooking potatoes. Good, I think, with some spicy little Italian sausages, or another suggestion from a friend who tried this was to top the potato with fried eggs and grated cheese and then flash it under the grill.

½ lb (225 g) red or green peppers
1 lb (450 g) potatoes
2½ tablespoons olive oil
1 clove garlic (crushed)
1 medium onion (finely chopped)

½ lb (225 g) red ripe tomatoes (peeled and chopped) or 1 × 8 oz tin of Italian tomatoes (225 g)
Salt and freshly-milled black pepper

To serve
1 teaspoon chopped parsley (or 1 tablespoon fresh chopped basil leaves)

For this you need a large frying-pan with some sort of lid that will cover the ingredients while you cook them.

Begin by chopping the pepper into ¾ inch (20 mm) squares. Then peel and chop the potatoes into roughly ½ inch (15 mm) cubes and dry them as much as possible in a clean teacloth.

Now heat the oil in the frying-pan and soften the onion and pepper in it for 5 minutes, add the garlic and cook for a further minute. Then turn the heat up to high and add the potatoes. Toss them around in the oil for about 5 minutes, then pour in the tomatoes and a good seasoning of salt and freshly-milled black pepper. Turn the heat down to very low and put a lid on the pan and cook slowly for 40 minutes.

Serve sprinkled with some chopped parsley, or, if you are lucky enough to have some, fresh chopped basil leaves.

American Hashed Browns

Serves 4 – 6 people

Recipe sent by
David Bazant
Sunbury-on-Thames
Surrey

This is described by its contributor as 'heavenly'. What it is is a crisp cake made with grated potatoes flavoured with onion, pepper and a dash of chilli sauce and served with crumbled crisp bacon.

6 medium sized potatoes, approx. 2 lb (900 g) (peeled and cut in half)
4 rashers streaky bacon
1 medium onion (finely chopped)
1 small green pepper (finely chopped)
1 teaspoon chilli sauce (bottled)
Salt and freshly-milled black pepper
2 tablespoons butter

Bring a large saucepan of lightly salted water to the boil and boil the potatoes uncovered until they can be pierced with the tip of a small knife, about 10 minutes. Then drain the potatoes and leave them until they are cool enough to handle. Grate the potatoes on a coarse cheese grater into a large bowl. Add the onion and pepper and combine these with the grated potatoes using 2 large forks. Sprinkle with chilli sauce, mix and season with salt and freshly-milled black pepper.

Now, in a 10 inch (25 cm) frying-pan, preferably with a good non-stick surface, cook the bacon until it has rendered all of its fat and is crisp and brown, then remove it and drain on kitchen paper. Now add the butter to the bacon fat and place over the heat until the butter melts.

Add the potatoes and press them down firmly into the pan using a spatula. Cook them over a low to medium heat, shaking the pan occasionally to prevent the potatoes from sticking. A brown crust should form on the bottom surface of the potatoes in about 20 minutes, you can check this by raising the edge of the potatoes with the spatula. If necessary, cook for a few minutes longer, raising the heat to achieve the proper crispness. To serve, cover the frying-pan with a heated plate and, grasping the pan and the plate together, turn it upside down. The potatoes should fall out easily. Crumble the bacon into small pieces and sprinkle them over the potatoes.

Spinach Terrine with a Coulis of Tomatoes

Recipe sent by Captain M G Haworth Godalming Surrey

Serves 8 – 10 people

Captain Haworth says he first ate this terrine in a private house in Brittany – and certainly it conjures up dreams of hot summer days in France. But it would be perfect for a summer lunch party on either side of the Channel. I like it served with a coulis of tomatoes and I've included the recipe.

2 lb (900 g) fresh spinach leaves (cooked, drained and chopped) or 1 lb (450 g) frozen spinach (defrosted and drained)
8 eggs
½ pint (275 ml) double cream
8 oz (225 g) grated Gruyère cheese
2 tablespoons fresh chopped parsley
1 teaspoon fresh chopped basil (or thyme)
Salt and freshly-milled black pepper

Pre-heat oven to gas mark 7, 425°F (220°C).
You will also need a well-buttered terrine or loaf tin measuring 9 by 5 inches (23 by 13 cm) and 2 inches (5 cm) deep.

This is extremely simple to make: all you do is beat the eggs with a fork in a large mixing bowl and season them with salt and pepper. Then beat in the cream, followed by the cheese, chopped spinach, parsley and herbs.

When everything is thoroughly combined pour the mixture into the terrine. Half fill a meat roasting tin with warm water, place the terrine in it and bake in the oven for 30–40 minutes or until set. Then remove it from the oven, take it out of the water and leave in a cool place for 24 hours. Serve cut in slices with a tomato coulis, made as follows.

Tomato Coulis

2 lb (900 g) tomatoes (skinned and sliced with seeds removed)
2 tablespoons olive oil
2 medium onions (thinly sliced)

For the vinaigrette dressing
1 tablespoon wine vinegar
½ teaspoon mustard powder
½ teaspoon salt
1 clove of garlic (crushed)
3 tablespoons olive oil
Freshly-milled black pepper

Heat the 2 tablespoons of olive oil in a pan then gently sweat the onions till just soft. Add the prepared tomatoes and gently stir them around over a low heat until they soften a little. They mustn't start to go mushy – 5 minutes cooking is about all they need. Now pour them into a shallow serving dish and make up the dressing (simply place all the ingredients in a screw-top jar and shake it vigorously to amalgamate everything). Sprinkle it over the tomatoes, leave to cool, and chill till needed.

Chinese Green Vegetable Salad

Recipe sent by Caroline Liddell London N7

Serves 4 people

This is very green and pretty to look at. The vegetables are lightly cooked and then tossed in a spicy Chinese dressing whilst still warm, enabling them to absorb all the lovely flavours.

8 oz (225 g) broccoli heads
8 oz (225 g) haricots verts
8 oz (225 g) mange-tout
6 little finger-thick spring onions
3 oz (75 g) tinned sliced water chestnuts or 2 oz (50 g) blanched almonds, cut into slivers and toasted
1 tablespoon sesame seeds

For the dressing
2 tablespoons thick soy sauce
4 tablespoons olive oil
1 tablespoon medium-dry sherry
1 teaspoon sugar
1 clove garlic (finely chopped)
2 teaspoons fresh ginger (grated or finely chopped)
Freshly-milled black pepper

Begin by preparing the vegetables. First cut the individual broccoli florets from the stalks – you need small florets, about the size of a 5 pence coin. Reserve only the tender upper parts of the main stalks and cut these obliquely into slices, ⅛ to ¼ inch thick (3 to 5 mm).

Next top and tail the haricots and mange-tout, then cut the haricots into 1 inch (2.5 cm) lengths and slice the mange-tout obliquely into diamond-shaped strips. Now cut the white parts of the spring onions in the same way and finally cut the water chestnuts into slivers.

Next make the dressing by putting all the ingredients into a small bowl and whisking them together with a fork.

Pour a kettle full of boiling water (about 3 pints or 1.7 litres) into a large saucepan. Add a teaspoon of salt and bring this back to the boil.

Boil the broccoli for exactly 3 minutes, then remove it to a colander with a draining spoon and drain it thoroughly. Now transfer the broccoli to a mixing bowl, then cook the haricots in the boiling water for 2 minutes. Add the mange-tout and cook with the beans for a further 1½ minutes.

Now drain both thoroughly and combine all the vegetables (including the prepared onions and water chestnuts or almonds) and then pour the dressing over everything. Stir gently, cover and cool. Serve the salad at room temperature, sprinkled with the sesame seeds. This is extremely good with cold or grilled chicken or fish.

Italian Broad Bean and Mushroom Salad

Serves 6 people

Recipe sent by Susan Fancourt Ross-on-Wye Hereford

This is essentially a salad for summer, when the broad beans are young and green but you could use frozen beans during the winter.

1 lb (450 g) broad beans (shelled weight) lightly cooked
6 oz (175 g) mushrooms (wiped and sliced)
1 large Spanish onion, about 10 oz (275 g) in weight (peeled and chopped)
2 tablespoons freshly chopped parsley
1 tablespoon freshly chopped basil (or in winter 1 level teaspoon dried oregano)

For the dressing
¼ pint (150 ml) white wine vinegar
3 fl. oz (75 ml) olive oil
2 cloves of garlic (crushed)
Salt and freshly-milled black pepper
Celery salt

In a large salad bowl combine the beans, mushrooms, onion and herbs. Then simply place the vinegar, oil, garlic and seasonings to taste in a screw-top jar and shake vigorously.

Pour the dressing over the salad and toss everything to get it completely coated in dressing. Now leave the salad in a cool place for several hours for the flavours to develop and become absorbed.

Serve the salad with some French bread and salami and a bottle of something Italian!

Pasta Salad with Broccoli and Anchovies

Serves 6–8 people

Recipe sent by
Connie Harman
London SW9

This is a recipe from America – where so many different kinds of pasta salads abound. Here's a particularly colourful one, full of flavour. Mrs Harman recommends using a really good virgin olive oil.

12 oz (350 g) pasta (bows, shells or wheels)
1 lb (450 g) broccoli heads
1 × 1¾ oz (45 g) tin of anchovies in oil
2 teaspoons finely chopped garlic (2 cloves)
2 tablespoons fresh chopped parsley
2 tablespoons olive oil
Juice of 1 lemon
8 oz (225 g) small tomatoes (each cut into 6 wedges)
Salt and freshly-milled black pepper

First of all make up the dressing: drain the oil from the tin of anchovies into a large mixing bowl, then finely chop the anchovies and add these to the bowl along with the garlic and parsley. Next add the olive oil and lemon juice, then a little freshly-milled black pepper and mix well.

Cook the pasta in plenty of boiling salted water (with a few drops of oil added to keep it separate) for 8 minutes exactly, then drain in a colander and cool it under cold running water till quite cold. Then drain again. Now cut the broccoli heads down to individual florets no bigger than a 10p piece, and steam them (covered) over boiling water for a maximum of 5 minutes, probably less (they must retain a good deal of bite, so don't go away and forget about them).

Drain the broccoli and toss it in the dressing whilst still warm, then add the tomatoes and pasta, toss and mix everything thoroughly. Taste to check the seasoning and serve the salad at room temperature.

Mizeria (Polish Cucumber Salad)

Serves 3 or 4 people

Recipe sent by Mrs E Thiel-Cecrwinke Southend-on-Sea Essex

This recipe belies its name. Our sender describes it as 'delicious and refreshing' – not in the least bit like its gloomy name, which in English means misery.

1 large cucumber
1 teaspoon salt
4 fl. oz (110 ml) soured cream
Juice of ½ lemon
½ teaspoon caster sugar
½ teaspoon dried dillweed
Freshly-milled black pepper

First peel the cucumber, preferably with a potato peeler, then thinly slice it and place in a colander, sprinkling salt between the layers. Then stand the colander on a plate and leave it for about 1 hour to drain.

Meanwhile, mix the cream with the lemon juice, caster sugar, dillweed and a good seasoning of freshly-milled black pepper. Now, using your hands, squeeze out a handful of cucumber slices at a time and transfer them to a serving dish. Then pour the cream mixture over them and mix lightly to coat all the cucumber with the cream – taste to check the seasoning. Cover the cucumber and chill it lightly until ready to serve.

This is very good served as a side salad with fish or spicy Polish sausage.

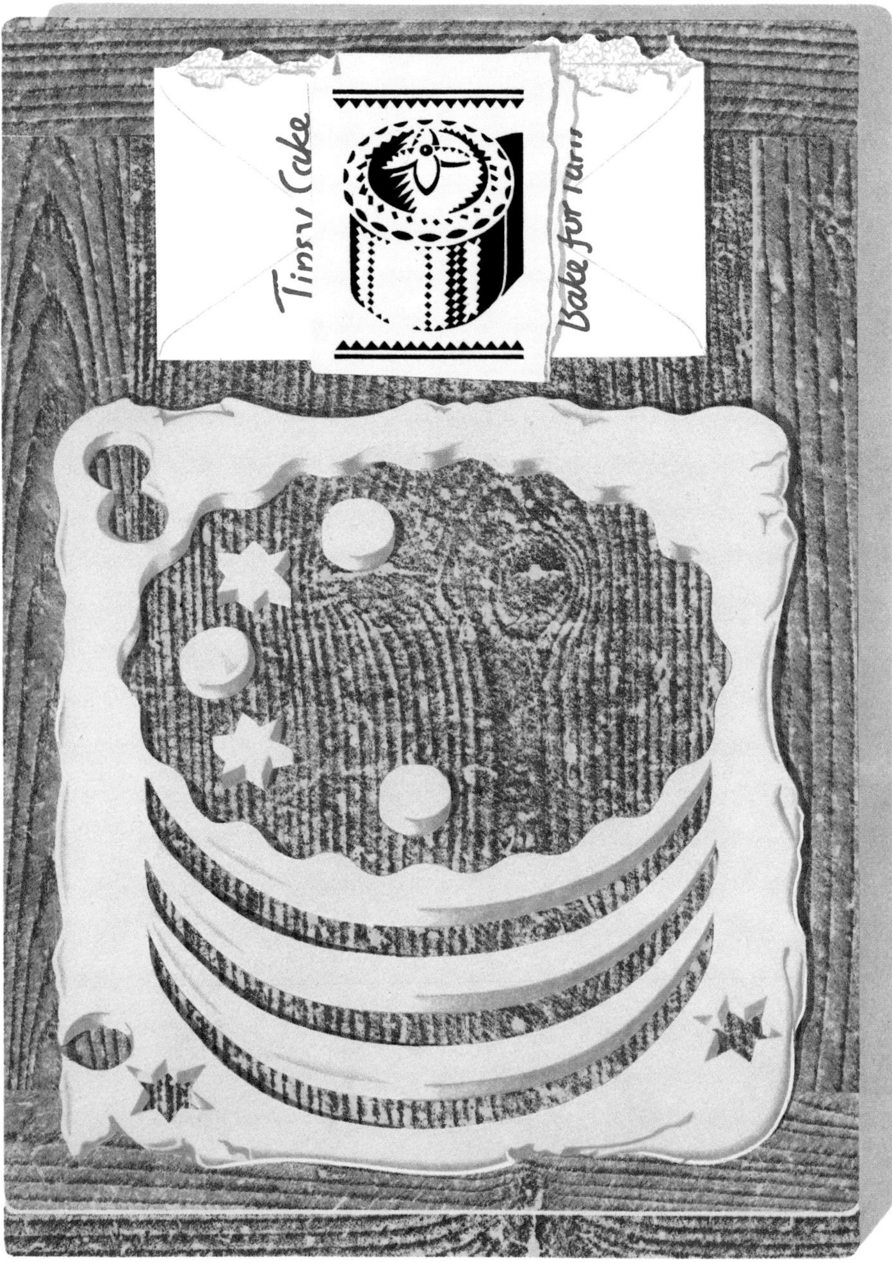
Cake
Bake for

BAKING

Quick Crunchy Brown Bread

Recipe sent by Sr Kathleen O'Sullivan Newmarket Cambridgeshire

Serves 6 people

If ever I go to Ireland the one thing I long to bring back is barrowloads of lovely Irish bread! Well, this is the nicest recipe for it I've come across this side of the Irish Sea.

6 oz (175 g) wholemeal flour
2 oz (50 g) plain flour
1 oz (25 g) pinhead oatmeal
1 oz (25 g) wheatgerm
1 oz (25 g) bran
1 teaspoon bicarbonate of soda
½ teaspoon salt
1 teaspoon sugar
1 egg
½ pint (275 ml) buttermilk (available at health food stores or supermarkets)

Pre-heat oven to gas mark 5, 375°F (190°C).
You will need 1 well-greased 1 lb (450 g) loaf tin.

Place the dry ingredients in a large, roomy bowl, then beat the egg and buttermilk together and add to the dry ingredients.

Mix first with a fork then finish off with your hands, to form a smooth dough. Transfer the dough to the tin, level the top and bake in the centre of the oven for 50–60 minutes. Turn it straight out onto a wire rack to cool.

Denis Law's Afternoon Tea Scone

Recipe sent by Denis Law

Makes a 9 inch round scone

Hot and fresh from the oven, and spread with homemade jam – what nicer treat could there be for a winter's weekend (or after a hard game of football)?

9 oz (250 g) plain flour
1 teaspoon baking powder
7 oz (200 g) granulated sugar
2 oz (50 g) margarine
5 oz (150 g) raisins
1 (size 2) egg
4 fl. oz (110 ml) milk

Pre-heat oven to gas mark 6, 400°F (200°C).
You will need 1 well greased 8½ or 9 inch (21 or 23 cm) round cake tin.

First, place the flour, baking powder and sugar in a large mixing bowl. Then rub in the margarine until the mixture resembles fine breadcrumbs. After that stir in the raisins to distribute them evenly.

Now in a small bowl beat together the egg and milk and add this (reserving 1 dessertspoon) to the rest of the ingredients. Then mix to a soft, slightly sticky dough (you may or may not need the remaining liquid). Turn the dough out on to a floured surface, knead it briefly and lightly to form a round, then transfer it to the tin. Using the flat of your hand push the dough out evenly to the size of the tin. Then bake it in the top half of the oven for 45 minutes. Serve warm and fresh from the oven, cut into slices and spread with butter and preserves.

Ginger Biscuits

Makes 24 biscuits

Recipe sent by
Mary Aaron
Darlington
Co Durham

This recipe is supplied by a friend of mine at my request as I think they are the nicest ginger biscuits I've ever tasted.

5 oz (150 g) golden syrup
4 oz (110 g) margarine
12 oz (350 g) plain flour
10 oz (275 g) sugar
2 teaspoons powdered ginger
1 teaspoon bicarbonate of soda
1 egg
A pinch of salt

Pre-heat oven to gas mark 4, 350°F (180°C).
You will also need 2 well-greased baking sheets.

The best way to weigh golden syrup is to weigh a small saucepan first, then spoon the syrup in up to the required weight. Then add the margarine to the saucepan and melt the two together.

Now sift the flour, sugar, salt, ginger and bicarbonate of

soda into a mixing bowl, then beat the egg and stir that and the syrup mixture into the dry ingredients. Mix well until you have a smooth dough.

Then take rounded teaspoonfuls of the mixture and roll them into small rounds, put these on to the baking sheets, allowing room for spreading, and bake them for 15 minutes. Then let them cool completely on the baking sheet before removing and storing in an airtight tin.

Wholewheat Oatcakes

Recipe sent by Margaret Rittman Stanford-le-Hope Essex

Makes 28 cakes

These are lovely with cheese and for me they help to make a cheese course at a dinner party into something a bit more special than the shop-bought cheese biscuits I get very bored with.

7 oz (200 g) oatmeal (fine or coarse porridge oats will do)
4 oz (110 g) wholewheat flour
½ teaspoon salt
1 teaspoon baking powder
1 oz (25 g) caster sugar
3 oz (75 g) margarine
1 egg (beaten)
Milk to bind

Pre-heat oven to gas mark 4, 350°F (180°C).

Begin by putting the oats, flour, salt, baking powder and sugar into a bowl and then rub in the margarine. In another small bowl mix together the egg and 1 tablespoon of milk with a fork, then add sufficient of this mixture to bind the oat mixture to a dough (you probably won't need all of it).

Now sprinkle a surface with some wholewheat flour and roll the dough to ⅛ inch (3 mm) thick, then using a 2¾ inch (7 cm) plain cutter, cut out the biscuits (because of the porridge oats you'll need to give each one a very sharp tap to cut through it neatly). Then re-roll the pastry trimmings, using the egg/milk mixture to moisten if necessary.

Bake the biscuits in the oven for 20–25 minutes. These store very well in an airtight tin.

Icelandic Curly Peters

To make 3 – 4 dozen

Recipe sent by
Mrs D. E. Macara
Milton Keynes
Bucks

The secret of these little biscuits is to eat them crisp and fresh – they tend to disappear very quickly anyway. However, if you pop them into an airtight tin as soon as they are cold, you can re-crisp them in the oven later if you feel they need it.

8 oz (225 g) moist brown sugar
8 oz (225 g) butter or margarine (at room temperature)
1 egg
1 tablespoon warmed syrup
1 teaspoon cinnamon
4 oz (110 g) chopped walnuts
4 oz (110 g) raisins
8 oz (225 g) self-raising flour

Pre-heat the oven to gas mark 4, 350°F (180°C).
You'll also need two large baking sheets (greased).

First of all, cream the butter and sugar together till you have a pale, fluffy dropping consistency, then break in the whole egg and add the syrup. Stir these in, using a wooden spoon, until the mixture is quite smooth.

Now sift in the flour and cinnamon, and gradually fold this in, finally adding the walnuts and raisins. Then drop rounded teaspoonfuls of the mixture on to the baking sheets – about 10 on each one (this won't use up all the mixture, but see below).

Bake this first batch of biscuits for about 20 minutes, during which time they will have spread out quite a bit. Take them out of the oven, then after a couple of minutes remove them from the baking sheets to a cooling tray. Then finish off the rest of the mixture as above.

Oat and Fruit Nutties

Makes 16 – 18 biscuits

Recipe sent by
Margaret Parker
Dudley
West Midlands

These 'full of goodness' little biscuits are so quick and easy to make and lovely to eat.

4 oz (110 g) porridge oats
2½ oz (60 g) mixed dried fruit
1 oz (25 g) chopped nuts (any kind, walnuts, hazelnuts, etc)
2½ oz (60 g) soft brown sugar
3 oz (75 g) flour
¼ teaspoon salt
5 oz (150 g) butter or margarine
1 rounded teaspoon golden syrup
½ teaspoon bicarbonate of soda
2 tablespoons boiling water
2 teaspoons wine or cider vinegar

Pre-heat oven to gas mark 4, 350°F (180°C).

Sift the flour and salt into a mixing bowl, then add the oats, dried fruit, nuts and sugar and mix well.

Then in a small saucepan gently melt the butter and syrup together. While this is happening mix the bicarbonate of soda in a cup with 2 tablespoons of boiling water.

Now stir the melted fat and syrup into the dry ingredients, followed by the water mixture, followed by the vinegar. Mix thoroughly and simply drop teaspoonfuls of the mixture onto 2 greased baking trays. Bake the biscuits in the centre of the oven for 25–30 minutes.

Dame Kiri Te Kanawa's Anzac Biscuits

Makes about 3½ dozen biscuits

Recipe sent by Dame Kiri Te Kanawa

Dame Kiri's little coconut-flavoured biscuits from down under are straightforward, quick to make and quite delicious.

4 oz (110 g) plain flour
6 oz (175 g) granulated sugar
3 oz (75 g) desiccated coconut
3 oz (75 g) rolled oats (we used porridge oats)
3½ oz (85 g) butter
1 tablespoon golden syrup
½ teaspoon bicarbonate of soda
2 tablespoons boiling water

Pre-heat oven to gas mark 4, 350°F (180°C).
You'll also need 2 well-greased baking sheets.

Start off by combining the flour, sugar, coconut and oats in a mixing bowl. Then place the butter in a small pan along with the syrup and warm these gently until melted, then remove from the heat.

Next dissolve the bicarbonate of soda in the boiling water in a cup, stir this into the melted butter-and-syrup mixture, and then stir the whole lot into the dry ingredients until the mixture forms a stiff paste. Now arrange walnut-sized lumps of the paste on the greased baking sheets – about 1 inch (2.5 cm) apart to allow room for expansion – and bake in the oven for 15 minutes.

Leave the biscuits on the trays for a minute or two before using a palette knife to loosen them. Cool them on wire racks and store in an airtight tin

Cinnamon and Date Slices

Recipe sent by
Mrs Edmonds
Stanley
Co Durham

Makes 16 slices

You could, if you wanted to, use another filling for this – chopped dried apricots or figs. Anyway, it is really delicious with dates.

8 oz (225 g) dates (chopped small)
1 tablespoon honey
5 tablespoons water
1 tablespoon lemon juice
1 level teaspoon ground cinnamon
6 oz (175 g) butter or margarine (at room temperature)
3 oz (75 g) caster sugar
6 oz (175 g) semolina
6 oz (175 g) wholemeal self-raising flour, or plain wholemeal and 1 level teaspoon baking powder

Pre-heat oven to gas mark 3, 325°F (170°C).
You will need a greased tin, 11 by 7 inches, 1 inch deep (28 by 18 cm, 2.5 cm deep).

First put the dates, honey, water, lemon juice and cinnamon in a saucepan and heat them gently until the honey dissolves. Then stir with a wooden spoon until you have a good creamy consistency. Then remove the pan from the heat.

Cream together the butter and caster sugar until pale and creamy, stir in the semolina and flour and mix well until the mixture resembles fine breadcrumbs.

Now press half of this mixture into the greased tin and then spread the date mixture evenly over that, and lastly sprinkle the rest of the shortbread mixture over the dates, pressing it all down lightly. Bake in the oven for 40–45 minutes or until golden brown, and then mark them into 16 fingers whilst they are still warm and leave to cool in the tin before removing.

Linzertorte

Recipe sent by Mrs A Russell Tonbridge Kent

To make a 9 inch (23 cm) cake

This is a beautiful version of the famous tart or cake that originated in the town of Linz in Austria. The crust is very rich – half cake and half pastry made with almonds. It is quite difficult to roll out, but responds well to being eased out with your fingers and the flat of a tablespoon.

6 oz (175 g) flour
1/8 teaspoon ground cloves
1/4 teaspoon ground cinnamon
6 oz (175 g) unblanched almonds (finely ground in a food processor or liquidiser)
4 oz (110 g) sugar
1 teaspoon grated lemon zest
2 hard boiled egg yolks (mashed)
8 oz (225 g) unsalted butter (at room temperature)
2 raw egg yolks (lightly beaten)
1 teaspoon vanilla essence
a 12 oz (350 g) jar of thick raspberry jam
icing sugar (sieved)

To serve
Double cream, whipped and chilled

Pre-heat the oven to gas mark 4, 350 °F (180 °C).
You'll also need a 9 inch (23 cm) cake tin with removable base, lightly buttered.

Begin by beating the butter with a wooden spoon to soften it to the consistency of soft margarine. Next sift the flour, cloves and cinnamon into a deep mixing bowl, then add the almonds, sugar, lemon peel and mashed, hard boiled yolks.

Now, using a wooden spoon, beat in the butter, beaten raw egg yolks and vanilla essence. Continue to beat until the mixture is smooth and doughy. Form the dough into a ball, put it in a polythene bag or wrapping and refrigerate it for at least an hour or until firm.

Remove about three-quarters of the dough from the wrapping and return the rest to the 'fridge. Now roll out the dough lightly and carefully; as it's tricky to handle do the best you can, then transfer it to the tin, and ease it out with your hands and the back of a tablespoon to cover the base and to bring it about 1½ inches up the sides.

Now carefully spread the jam over the base. The remaining dough will be easier as this has only to be rolled out into thin strips and cut to arrange in a criss-cross pattern over the jam.

Bake the torte in the centre of the oven for 50 – 60 minutes: it should be lightly browned. Then remove from the oven, place the tin over a large jar and slip down the outside rim. After 5 minutes sprinkle with a generous dusting of icing sugar, then let the cake cool to room temperature before serving with chilled whipped cream.

Cranberry jelly makes a lovely alternative to raspberry jam.

Chocolate Chip and Walnut Cake

Makes 8 – 10 slices

Recipe sent by
Mary Wren
Wetherby
W Yorkshire

Experience has shown that this very simple cake is extremely popular with children (and no less so with grown ups!).

4 oz (110 g) wholemeal flour
4 oz (110 g) plain white flour
3 teaspoons baking powder
4 oz (110 g) butter or margarine (room temperature)
4 oz (110 g) soft brown sugar
2 eggs (beaten)
4 tablespoons milk
2 tablespoons clear honey
2 oz (50 g) chopped walnuts
2 oz (50 g) chocolate chips

Pre-heat oven to gas mark 4, 350°F (180°C).
You will also need a 2 lb (900 g) loaf tin greased and lined.

First, sieve the flours and baking powder into a mixing bowl, and then add the bits of bran remaining in the sieve.

Rub in the butter to the crumbly stage and then add the sugar, eggs, milk and honey and beat the mixture well. Lastly stir in the walnuts and chocolate chips and then pour the mixture into the prepared tin. Bake for 1 – 1¼ hours until firm to the touch. Leave it to cool in the tin for 15 minutes before turning out. Allow to cool completely before slicing.

Wholewheat Chocolate Hazelnut Cake

Recipe sent by
Gilda Naumann
Uley Dursley
Gloucestershire

Makes 12 – 16 slices

This is a lovely cake which disappears like lightning!

6 oz (175 g) butter or margarine
6 oz (175 g) golden granulated sugar
3 eggs (beaten)
2 tablespoons milk
6 oz (175 g) wholemeal flour (sifted)
2½ level teaspoons baking powder
7 oz (200 g) plain dessert chocolate (chopped quite small)
4 oz (110 g) ground hazelnuts
1 oz (25 g) chopped hazelnuts

Pre-heat oven to gas mark 4, 350°F (180°C).
You will need a 7 inch (18 cm) greased and lined deep, round cake tin.

First, cream together the butter and sugar until pale, light and fluffy. Then add the eggs, a little at a time, beating well between each addition. Now fold in the milk, sifted flour and baking powder and fold and mix them well. Now add the chocolate pieces together with the ground hazelnuts and then spoon the mixture into the prepared tin.

Finally sprinkle over the chopped hazelnuts and bake the cake in the centre of the oven for about 1½ hours, or until the centre is springy when lightly touched. After 1 hour, cover the cake with a sheet of greaseproof paper to prevent the nuts browning too much. Leave the cake to cool in the tin for 5 – 10 minutes before turning out.

Chocolate Nut-Coated Cherry Cake

Recipe sent by Mrs J Halfpenny Bromsgrove Worcestershire

Makes 18 squares

Here's a very quick and easy recipe to make – but it does need to be done well in advance as the chocolate coating should be completely set before you remove it from the tin.

8 oz (225 g) plain dessert chocolate
1½ oz (40 g) chopped mixed nuts
4 oz (110 g) butter or margarine (room temperature)
8 oz (225 g) caster sugar
2 large eggs
½ teaspoon vanilla essence
8 oz (225 g) rolled oats
4 oz (110 g) glacé cherries (cut into quarters)
4 oz (110 g) raisins

You will also need a cake tin measuring 11 by 7 inches, 2 inches deep (28 by 18 cm, 5 cm deep), greased and lined with greaseproof paper also lightly greased.

Begin by melting the chocolate: break it up into squares and place it in a bowl set over a pan of hot (but not boiling) water, leave for a few minutes then stir till melted down to a liquid. Now simply pour the chocolate into the base of the prepared tin and sprinkle the chopped nuts evenly all over the melted chocolate. Then allow it to cool and set hard.

After that you can make the cake. Pre-heat the oven to gas mark 3, 325 °F (170 °C), then cream the butter or margarine with the sugar until pale and fluffy. Next whip up the eggs with the vanilla essence and mix them into the creamed mixture, a little at a time, beating well after each addition.

Now fold in first the oats, then the cherries and raisins. Mix well, then spread the cake mixture all over the chocolate base and bake the cake for 40 minutes or until golden brown. Leave it to cool for 5 minutes, then cut it into squares in the tin, but leave until the chocolate has cooled and set again before removing from the tin.

New Zealand Moist Carrot Cake

To make an 8 inch (20 cm) cake

Recipe sent by
Yolanda Couchman
Virginia Water
Surrey

In my capacity as a cookery writer I have come across a fair amount of carrot cakes in my time but this one wins the crown – it is simply superlative!

9 oz (250 g) wholemeal flour
6 oz (175 g) raw sugar (muscovado or Barbados)
6 oz (175 g) soft brown sugar
3 × size three eggs
6 fl. oz (175 ml) sunflower oil
2 fl. oz (55 ml) soured cream
2 teaspoons pure vanilla essence
Approx. 1 teaspoon freshly-grated nutmeg
2 level teaspoons cinnamon
1 teaspoon bicarbonate of soda
½ teaspoon salt
11 oz (300 g) grated carrots
3 oz (75 g) desiccated coconut

For the topping
4 oz (110 g) full fat soft cream cheese
2 oz (50 g) unsalted butter
2 oz (50 g) sifted icing sugar
Juice of ½ lemon

Pre-heat oven to gas mark 2, 300°F (150°C).
You will need one 8 inch (20 cm) round cake tin (lined with greaseproof paper) and two mixing bowls.

In the first mixing bowl you place the eggs, oil, vanilla essence and soured cream, then sieve the sugars into it as well (to avoid any lumps). Into the other bowl you sift the flour, nutmeg, cinnamon, soda and salt.

Now beat the wet ingredients and the sugars together, then fold in the dry ingredients, followed by the carrots and coconut. Mix well to distribute everything evenly, then spoon into the cake tin and bake on the centre shelf for 1½ to 2 hours.

When the cake is cool mix the topping ingredients together and spread thickly all over the top.

Previous page, left to right: Icelandic Curly Peters page 131; New Zealand Moist Carrot Cake; Oat and Fruit Nutties page 131; Linzertorte page 134.

Fresh Plum Cake

Serves 8 people

Recipe sent by
Elizabeth Sargut
Reading
Berkshire

Elizabeth Sargut describes this as a 'deliciously moist cake that lasts for ages' – she says all her friends have asked for the recipe. Perhaps now she can sell them all this book!

12 oz (350 g) self-raising flour
½ teaspoon salt
2 teaspoons cinnamon
6 oz (175 g) hard margarine
3 oz (75 g) + 2 tablespoons soft brown sugar
3 oz (75 g) sultanas
1 lb (450 g) fresh plums
6 tablespoons golden syrup
3 eggs

Pre-heat oven to gas mark 4, 350°F (180°C).
You will need an 8 inch (20 cm) round cake tin, greased and lined.

First, sift the flour, salt and 1 teaspoon of cinnamon into a large mixing bowl. Add the margarine and cut it into small pieces with a sharp knife. Then discard the knife and rub it in with your fingertips until you get a mixture that resembles breadcrumbs. Now stir in the 3 oz (75 g) brown sugar and sultanas.

Next cut the plums into halves, discard the stones and then reserve 10 complete halves and chop the rest finely. After that put the golden syrup and eggs into a bowl and beat them gently. Now add this mixture to the dry ingredients and then fold in the chopped plums. Next, spoon the mixture into the cake tin and level it with the back of a spoon, then arrange the sliced plum halves on the top.

Finally, mix the remaining 2 tablespoons of brown sugar and 1 teaspoon of cinnamon and sprinkle over the top of the cake. Bake in the centre of the oven for approx. 2 hours. To test if it is cooked press the centre lightly with your fingers – if it is cooked it will not leave an impression. Leave the cake to cool completely in the tin before turning it out. Then wrap it up in foil and leave it for 2 days to mature. It will keep for at least a week and will taste better every day!

Brown Ale Loaf Cake

Makes one 2 lb loaf

Recipe sent by
Mrs B Wolstencroft
Warrington
Lancashire and
Mrs C E Moseley
Milton Keynes
Buckinghamshire

Mrs Wolstencroft and Mrs Moseley say this recipe was handed down by their mother, Ciss, who always made large quantities of it at Christmas and gave one to each member of the family.

4 oz (110 g) butter or margarine (at room temperature)
4 oz (110 g) soft brown sugar
1 tablespoon treacle
Grated zest of ½ orange
2 eggs (lightly beaten)
8 oz (225 g) plain flour
1 level teaspoon mixed spice
½ level teaspoon ground nutmeg
12 oz (350 g) mixed dried fruit
1 oz (25 g) chopped mixed peel
2 oz (50 g) walnuts (chopped)
1 tablespoon rum
3 fl. oz (75 ml) brown ale

Pre-heat oven to gas mark 2, 300°F (150°C).
You'll also need a 2 lb (900 g) loaf tin, lined and greased.

In a large mixing bowl cream the butter and sugar together until it's pale, light and fluffy, then beat in the treacle and orange zest. Next add the eggs, a little at a time, beating well after each addition, and after that fold in the sifted flour and spices followed by the fruit, peel and walnuts.

Lastly add the rum and brown ale and continue to fold all this in carefully. Spoon the mixture into the loaf tin, level off the surface and bake in the oven for 1 hour. After that reduce the temperature to gas mark 1, 275°F (140°C) and cook for a further 1¾ hours. During the final 45 minutes of the cooking time cover the loaf with a double thickness of greaseproof paper to prevent the top from burning. Leave to cool in the tin for a while before turning out on to a wire tray to get quite cold.

Rich Drambuie Fruit Cake

Makes 20 – 24 slices

Recipe sent by
Iain MacDonald
Warminster
Wiltshire

This is a very dark, rich, moist fruit cake that would be a good choice for Christmas or some other celebration.

For the fruit mixture
6 oz (175 g) chopped glacé cherries (pre-soak in hot water for a minute to remove syrup)
6 oz (175 g) chopped mixed peel
1 lb (450 g) sultanas
1 lb (450 g) raisins
12 oz (350 g) currants
3 tablespoons (1 miniature bottle) Drambuie

For the cake
10 oz (275 g) butter at room temperature
10 oz (275 g) soft brown sugar
6 eggs (beaten)
1 tablespoon black treacle
7 oz (200 g) wholewheat flour
3 oz (75 g) bran
¼ whole nutmeg (grated)
1 teaspoon cinnamon
¼ teaspoon powdered cloves
¼ teaspoon powdered mace
3 oz (75 g) chopped nuts (walnuts, brazils or any kind)
3 tablespoons Drambuie

You will need a 10 inch (25.5 cm) round cake tin, greased and lined with double greaseproof paper and also a double thickness of brown paper tied round the outside of the tin.

The night before you make the cake assemble the fruit mixture in a bowl, sprinkle the Drambuie over and mix well. Then cover the whole lot and leave to soak overnight.

Next day pre-heat oven to gas mark 1, 275°F (140°C).

In your largest mixing bowl begin the cake by creaming the butter and sugar together until pale, light and fluffy. Then beat in the eggs a little at a time (about a dessertspoon) until completely incorporated. Then mix in the black treacle.

Next fold in the flour, bran and spices and after that the fruit mixture and nuts. Finally fold in 3 more tablespoons of Drambuie and then spoon the mixture into the prepared tin. Level the surface and place a double square of greaseproof paper with a small hole in the centre (about the size of a 5p piece) over the cake and bake it in the oven, on a low shelf, for 4 hours and 15 minutes.

Allow to cool before taking it out of the tin. It keeps very well in an airtight tin and tastes better if it's kept a few days.

ALDER

PUDDINGS

Upside-Down Ginger Apple Pudding

Makes 12 – 16 slices

Recipe sent by
Mary Cox
Woolpit
Suffolk

This is for those who, like me, like very dark, sticky gingerbread. It can be served warm from the oven with custard or chilled pouring cream. Cool and store in an airtight tin for 24 hours to mature.

For the base
2 oz (50 g) butter or margarine (at room temperature)
3 oz (75 g) demerara sugar
1 tablespoon lemon juice
2 Bramley apples (12 oz or 350 g after peeling and coring)

For the gingerbread
1 lb (450 g) plain flour
8 oz (225 g) soft dark brown sugar
6 oz (175 g) butter or margarine
6 oz (175 g) black treacle
6 oz (175 g) golden syrup
(*Note:* instead of the golden syrup and black treacle, you could substitute 12 oz or 350 g of dark syrup)
3 slightly rounded teaspoons ground ginger
½ teaspoon cinnamon
2 teaspoons baking powder
½ teaspoon bicarbonate of soda
8 fl. oz (225 ml) milk
1 egg (beaten)

Pre-heat oven to gas mark 3, 325°F (170°C).
You will also need a tin or dish 8 by 12 inches, 2 inches deep (20 by 30 cm, 5 cm deep) and lined with baking parchment.

First cream together the butter and sugar along with the lemon juice. Then spread this mixture evenly over the lined baking tin. Next cut the peeled and cored apples into quarters, slice them very thinly and lay them all over the base

Now for the gingerbread. Sieve the flour, spices, baking powder and bicarbonate of soda together into a large mixing bowl. Then, in a saucepan, warm together the sugar, butter, treacle and syrup, being careful not to let the mixture get too hot. In another pan, warm the milk and beat the egg into it.

Now pour all the liquids into the flour and spices and mix everything very thoroughly. Then pour the mixture over the apples in the prepared tin and bake in the oven for 1 hour. Leave the gingerbread in the tin to cool for 30 minutes to allow the apple base to set. Then turn the cake out and carefully peel off the paper. What you will have is a sticky gingerbread topped with a caramelised apple purée.

German Apple Cake

Recipe sent by
Pauline Wheeler
Sanderstead
Surrey

Serves 8 people

This is probably nicest served hot as a dessert but it does taste very good cold. Either way we like it with chilled whipped cream or soured cream flavoured with a little cinnamon.

1 lb (450 g) cooking apples (peeled, cored and sliced)
4 oz (110 g) butter or margarine
4 oz (110 g) granulated sugar
8 oz (225 g) self-raising flour (sifted)
A pinch of salt
1 egg (beaten)
4 oz (110 g) sultanas
½ level teaspoon ground cinnamon
2 oz (50 g) demerara sugar
Icing sugar

Pre-heat oven to gas mark 5, 375 °F (190 °C).
You will need a 7 inch (18 cm) cake tin, well greased.

First of all melt the butter or margarine in a large saucepan, remove the pan from the heat and stir in the sugar, sifted self-raising flour, salt and egg and, using a wooden spoon, mix everything to a stiff, smooth dough.

Now place two-thirds of the dough into the greased cake tin and press it out as evenly as possible using your hands. Now, mix together the apples, sultanas and cinnamon and place these in the cake tin, all over the dough, then sprinkle over the demerara sugar and level the surface as much as possible using the back of a tablespoon. Now carefully spread the remaining dough over the apples.

Bake in the oven for 50–55 minutes or until the top is golden brown. Leave it to cool in the tin for 10 minutes before turning out and serving, sprinkled with icing sugar.

Apple Whisky Meringue

Serves 6 people

Recipe sent by
Mrs B. Mitchell
Padiham
Lancashire

This is a crisp flan filled with honey and whisky-flavoured apples and topped with a cloud of meringue.

6 oz (175 g) plain flour (sifted)
3½ oz (85 g) butter or margarine
6 oz (175 g) caster sugar
1 egg yolk and 2 egg whites
1 lb (450 g) cooking apples (peeled and cored)
1 tablespoon honey
1 tablespoon whisky

Pre-heat oven to gas mark 5, 375°F (190°C).

First make the pastry. Place the sifted flour in a bowl. Then rub in the butter until the mixture resembles fine breadcrumbs and after that mix in 2 oz (50 g) caster sugar. Now bind the mixture together with the egg yolk and enough cold water to make a smooth dough (about 1 tablespoon). Knead it lightly on a floured surface, then pop it into a polythene bag and let it rest for 15 minutes.

Roll the pastry out to line an 8 inch (20 cm) flan tin, prick the base all over and then chill the flan case in the fridge for 30 minutes before baking. Now cover the pastry with a sheet of greaseproof paper and add baking beans or dried peas and bake it blind in the oven for 15 minutes. After that, carefully remove the beans and paper and bake the flan for a further 10 minutes to dry it out completely.

While that is happening, roughly chop the apples and place them in a small saucepan with the honey and 1 tablespoon of water. Cover the pan and cook the apples gently for about 10–15 minutes or until they have collapsed and softened. Then beat in the whisky and spread the apple mixture into the flan case.

For the meringue, whisk the egg whites until they form soft peaks and gradually whisk in the remaining 4 oz (110 g) sugar. Then cover the apple mixture completely with the meringue, spreading it right up to the edges, and bake in the oven at gas mark 3, 325°F (170°C) for about 30 minutes until the meringue is pale beige and crisp.

Moist Chocolate Meringue Pudding

Recipe sent by Gail Pitcailbly

Serves 4 people

This is a sort of chocolate sponge only made with suet, hence the moist texture. It is then soaked in a chocolate sauce and topped with marshmallow meringue – certainly not one for diet days!

3 oz (75 g) self-raising flour
1 oz (25 g) cocoa powder
2 oz (50 g) shredded suet
2 oz (50 g) caster sugar
2 medium sized egg yolks
4 tablespoons milk

For the chocolate sauce
½ oz (10 g) butter
4 oz (110 g) plain chocolate
¼ pint (150 ml) milk

For the meringue topping
2 medium sized egg whites
2 oz (50 g) caster sugar
1 tablespoon granulated sugar

Pre-heat the oven to gas mark 6, 400°F (200°C).
You will need a buttered, 1½ pint (845 ml) ovenproof dish.

Begin by sifting the flour and cocoa together into a mixing bowl. Then add the suet and sugar and stir them lightly together. Next make a well in the centre and add the egg yolks and milk and mix to a soft consistency that will drop off a spoon easily. Now using a spatula scrape the mixture on to the prepared dish, level it out and then bake in the oven for just 20 minutes.

Meanwhile, make the sauce by placing the ingredients into a basin. Set the basin over hot (not boiling) water and allow the chocolate to melt, beating until smooth and shiny.

Remove the sponge from the oven and pour the sauce all over it. Then increase the oven temperature to gas mark 7, 425°F (220°C). Now whisk the egg whites for the topping until they form soft peaks (the peaks should stand up straight when the whisk is held up). Next fold in the caster sugar with light movements to keep the mixture well aerated. Do not stir.

Then simply spread the meringue on the top of the pudding, make peaks with the back of a spoon and sprinkle the granulated sugar all over the surface. Then return the pudding to the oven and bake for 2 to 5 minutes only, or until the meringue is just brown. Serve absolutely at once.

Date and Walnut Pudding with Brandy Syrup

Recipe sent by Linda Chick Ealing London

Serves 4 – 6 people

This is wickedly wonderful and, as its author says, 'It is an absolutely delicious combination of flavours and textures, enhanced with a liberal measure of booze!'

For the pudding
2 oz (50 g) butter or margarine
2 oz (50 g) caster sugar
1 egg (beaten)
4 oz (110 g) plain flour
1 teaspoon baking powder
2 oz (50 g) chopped walnuts
2½ oz (60 g) chopped dates
4 fl. oz (110 ml) boiling water
½ teaspoon bicarbonate of soda

For the syrup
2 oz (50 g) sugar
1 dessertspoon butter
3 fl. oz (75 ml) water
½ teaspoon vanilla essence
2 fl. oz (55 ml) brandy

Pre-heat oven to gas mark 5, 375°F (190°C).
You will need a 2 pint (1.25 litre) soufflé dish or pudding dish.

Start off by placing half the dates in a bowl, then pour the boiling water over them, add the bicarbonate of soda and leave aside until cool.

Meanwhile, cream the butter and sugar until pale, light and fluffy and then beat in the beaten egg a little at a time. Now sift the flour and baking powder and fold them into the rest by degrees, using a metal spoon. Next the nuts and the unsoaked dates are folded in, followed by the soaked dates along with the soaking water. Continue folding the mixture until everything is evenly distributed, then pour it into a well-greased cake tin and bake in the oven for 40 minutes.

Towards the end of the cooking time make the syrup. This you do by simply boiling together the sugar, butter and water for 5 minutes, then adding the vanilla essence and brandy.

When the pudding is cooked remove it from the oven and make some holes all over with a skewer. Pour the hot syrup on the pudding; it will be very quickly absorbed. Serve either hot or cold. It's quite delicious whichever way you choose. Linda recommends ice cream or dollops of chilled whipped cream as an accompaniment (sorry about the calories!).

Jamaican Planters' Pudding

Serves 6 – 8 people

Recipe sent by
Cynthia Clare Grant
Perth
Scotland

This recipe is, we think, quite stunning and would make a perfect ending to a very special dinner party – in Cynthia Clare Grant's words 'a subtle blend of coffee, fresh fruit, rum and cream'. It is based on a very old Jamaican recipe that appeared on the menu at Government House whenever royalty visited the island.

For the sponge
4 oz (110 g) butter (at room temperature)
4 oz (110 g) granulated sugar
3 eggs
3 tablespoons rum
4 oz (110 g) self-raising flour sifted with a pinch of salt
2 oz (50 g) maraschino cherries

For the filling
3 ripe bananas (but not soft)
Half a fresh pineapple
3 tablespoons Tia Maria
4 tablespoons Jamaican rum

For the topping
½ pint (275 ml) whipped cream
1 dozen maraschino cherries

Pre-heat the oven to gas mark 4, 350°F (180°C).

You will also need a 2 ½ pint (1.25 litre) ring mould (8 ¼ inches or 21 cm diameter) well-buttered and dusted with flour and a 3 ½ pint (2 litre) pudding bowl, well-buttered.

First separate the eggs, placing the yolks in a small bowl and the whites in a larger bowl. In a mixing bowl cream the butter and sugar until it's a very light and fluffy mixture. Stir the three tablespoons of rum into the egg yolks and beat lightly.

Using a clean dry whisk, whip up the egg whites until they form soft peaks. Now fold both the egg mixtures and the sifted flour into the creamed mixture alternately (each one a little bit at a time and in proportion). Finally, stir in the maraschino cherries.

Pour the cake mixture into the ring mould and bake for about 55 minutes. When it's cooked remove the cake to a cooling rack and leave it for 5 minutes or so before carefully loosening the sides with a palette knife and turning it out. Leave it to get quite cold on a wire rack.

Meanwhile, prepare the fruit filling: for this you need to slice the bananas fairly thinly and chop the pineapple into small dice. Then sprinkle half the rum over the fruit and leave it for one hour to soak up the flavour.

To assemble the pudding you need to cut the cake in half vertically. Now slice one half thinly into 26 slices and pop these on to a plate: slice the other half in the same way and put on a separate plate. Sprinkle one half with the Tia Maria.

Use the unsoaked slices to line the pudding basin over the base and sides, making sure that they overlap and that there are no gaps then sprinkle the remaining rum over the cake lining. Now into the centre put a layer of fruit, then a layer of soaked sponge, followed by another layer of fruit – and so on until everything is incorporated and you finish up with a layer of sponge on top. Now place a lightly buttered plate (buttered side down) on top of the pudding and press it down firmly.

Freeze the pudding for 24 hours, and remove it from the freezer 4 hours before serving. To serve, loosen the sides of the pudding with a palette knife, turn it out on to a plate, and decorate by covering it completely with the whipped cream and arranging the cherries on top.

Golden Soufflé Syrup Pudding

Serves 4 – 6 people

Recipe sent by
Celia Wreford
Bristol
Avon

This is a little gem of a pudding, such simple ingredients assembled and transformed into a luscious, golden surface covering a light soufflé centre over a pool of syrupy sauce – need we say more?

4 tablespoons of golden syrup
8 slices from a white loaf (cut medium thick)
2 oz (50 g) butter (room temperature)
2 eggs (beaten)
¾ pint (425 ml) milk

To serve
Lemon wedges
Chilled whipping cream

You will need a lightly buttered 3 pint deep baking dish. Pre-heat oven to gas mark 4, 350°F (180°C).

Begin by spooning the golden syrup all over the base of the baking dish.

Next, remove the crusts from the bread and butter the slices. Then cut each slice into 4 fingers and arrange these butter-side up on top of the syrup. Now whisk the eggs and milk together and pour this on top of the bread. Then place the pudding in the oven and bake for 40 to 50 minutes.

By this time it will be puffed up and golden brown. Serve speedily straight from the oven to the table, with lemon wedges and some chilled whipped cream.

Baked Almond, Honey and Apple Pudding

Serves 4 people

Recipe sent by
Hazel James
Seaford
Sussex

This is one of those hot English puddings that are such a rarity now that we are so calorie conscious, but once in a while it is very comforting to have a pudding like this one, served very hot with chilled pouring cream.

1 lb (450 g) cooking apples (weighed after peeling and coring)
1 tablespoon water
2–3 level tablespoons honey (depending on how sweet you like it)
3 oz (75 g) breadcrumbs
3 oz (75 g) butter or margarine
4 oz (110 g) demerara sugar
2 oz (50 g) ground almonds
1 egg (beaten)
Cream to serve

Pre-heat oven to gas mark 5, 375°F (190°C).
You will need 1 buttered, 2 pint (1.25 litre) baking dish.

Slice the apples straight into a saucepan, add the honey and the water and stew them gently until they are soft (this will take roughly 5 to 10 minutes). Then add the breadcrumbs to the apples and pour the mixture into a baking dish.

Next, rinse out the saucepan, dry it and add the butter and melt over a gentle heat, then take it off the heat and stir in the sugar and ground almonds and finally the beaten egg. Spread this mixture over the apple mixture and bake the pudding for 25–35 minutes, or until the top is a nice golden brown.

Hot Lemon Curd and Almond Tart

Serves 6 – 8 people

Recipe sent by
Mrs Isabel Purser
Inverness
Scotland

This is very good as a dessert, served with cream or custard. Sadly, most commercial lemon curds are unspeakable, so I've included a recipe for lemon curd here as well. If there's any of this left over, it tastes equally good cold.

Shortcrust pastry, made with 6 oz (175 g) flour and 3 oz (75 g) fat

For the topping
3 rounded tablespoons lemon curd
2 oz (50 g) butter or margarine
5 oz (150 g) semolina
5 oz (150 g) granulated sugar
1 teaspoon pure almond essence
1½ oz (40 g) almonds (finely chopped) or you could use ground almonds
1 egg (beaten)
1 teaspoon baking powder

You will need a baking tin (preferably non-stick) measuring 11 by 7 inches and 1½ inches deep (28 × 18 × 4 cm), lightly greased.
Pre-heat the oven to gas mark 4, 350°F (180°C) and pre-heat a baking sheet as well.

Roll out the pastry to an oblong large enough to line the tin, then spread the lemon curd all over the base. Place the tin in the refrigerator while you make up the topping.

This you do by melting the butter gently in a saucepan, then when it's melted remove from the heat, add the semolina, sugar, baking powder, almond essence and almonds. Finally, stir in the beaten egg, then carefully spread this mixture all over the lemon curd.

Bake the tart on the hot baking sheet on a high shelf in the oven for about 25 mintues. Then serve straightaway.

For a change, instead of almond essence, add the grated zest of half a lemon.

Fresh Lemon Curd

3 oz (75 g) caster sugar
1 large, juicy lemon (grated zest and juice)
2 large eggs
2 oz (50 g) unsalted butter

Place the grated lemon rind and sugar in a bowl. In another bowl whisk the lemon juice together with the eggs, then pour this mixture over the sugar. Add the butter cut into little pieces, and place the bowl over a pan of barely simmering water. Stir frequently till thickened – about 20 minutes.
Then cool the curd and use as required. Any left over can be stored in a screwtop jar.

Treacle and Roasted Hazelnut Tart

Serves 12 people

Recipe sent by
Beverley Dutton
Farnham
Surrey

This is much nicer and more special than the conventional treacle tart and it doesn't taste too sweet.

For the pastry
8 oz (225 g) plain flour
5 oz (150 g) butter
1 level tablespoon caster sugar
1 small egg (beaten)

For the filling and decoration
20 oz (550 g) golden syrup, or dark syrup (not black treacle)
8 oz (225 g) breadcrumbs (using 2 – 3 day old bread)
3 oz (75 g) roast hazelnuts (roughly chopped)
Juice and zest of 1 lemon
2 oz (50 g) roast hazelnuts for decorating
1 egg yolk (beaten with 1 dessertspoon of cold water for glazing)

Pre-heat oven to gas mark 5, 375 °F (190 °C).
You will need a 9 inch (23 cm) loose-bottomed flan tin, 1¼ inch (3 cm) deep and lightly greased.

Make the pastry in advance by sifting the flour and rubbing in the butter until the mixture resembles fine breadcrumbs. Then add the sugar followed by enough of the beaten egg to make a firm dough. Place the dough in a polythene bag and leave in the fridge for 1 hour. After that remove a quarter of the dough and keep aside, roll the rest out thinly to line the flan tin, then trim the edges and put the trimmings with the reserved pastry.

For the filling combine the syrup, breadcrumbs, chopped hazelnuts, lemon juice and zest in a bowl. Mix everything well and spoon it into the pastry case, spreading it out evenly.

Now roll out the reserved pastry and cut out strips approx. ¼ inch (5 mm) wide and lay these on top of the tart, spacing them about ½ inch (1 cm) apart making a lattice-work effect. Glaze the strips with the egg yolk and water, then bake on a baking sheet for 30 minutes or until the lattice-cross is golden brown. Pop a whole hazelnut into each lattice square. Beverley recommends at this stage drizzling a little warmed treacle over the whole thing to give the tart extra sparkle.

Autumn Pies

Makes about 1½ dozen

Recipe sent by Richard Bates and the boys and girls of Granton Primary School London SW16

According to 10-year-old Richard Bates who sent us this recipe 'from all the boys and girls of Granton School' they do a lot of cooking there, and made this recipe up themselves. You'll have to go and collect your own blackberries and elderberries in the autumn – but that's all part of the fun!

For the filling
1 cooking apple
4 oz (110 g) elderberries
4 oz (110 g) blackberries
2 oz (50 g) soft brown sugar
Approximately 1 tablespoon water

For the pastry
4 oz (110 g) margarine
4 oz (110 g) wholewheat flour
4 oz (110 g) plain white flour
A little milk (to glaze)
Sifted icing sugar (to serve)

Pre-heat the oven to gas mark 6, 400°F (200°C).
You will need two 2½ inch (6 cm) patty tins, one 3 inch (7.5 cm) and one 2½ inch (6 cm) fluted pastry cutter.

Make up the pastry by rubbing the fat into the flours until the mixture resembles breadcrumbs, then add just enough water to give you a dough that leaves the bowl clean. Pop it into a polythene bag and leave to rest in the fridge for 20 minutes or so.

Meanwhile, prepare the fruit. Quarter, core and peel the apple then slice it thinly straight into a saucepan. The elderberries and blackberries should be de-stalked, then rinsed and well drained. Now add the water to the apple in the pan, cover and cook over a very low heat until it is beginning to soften. At that point add the berries, cover the pan again and continue to cook for 3–5 minutes. Then remove from the heat, stir in the sugar gently and leave to cool.

Roll out half the pastry to a thickness of approximately ⅛ inch (3 mm) and use the 3 inch (7.5 cm) cutter to cut out 18 or so rounds (gathering up any scraps of pastry left and re-rolling them). Do the same with the other half of pastry, this time using the 2½ inch (6.5 cm) cutter. Now lightly grease the patty tins and line them with the larger rounds of pastry.

Place about 1 dessertspoon of the cooled fruit mixture into each pie, then dampen the edges of the smaller rounds of pastry with water and press them lightly into position to form lids on each pie, sealing the edges. Brush the tops with a little milk and make a small slit in each lid. Bake near the top of the oven for 25–30 minutes until they're a light golden-brown, then cool them on a wire tray and dust with icing sugar. Serve them warm or cold with cream.

Bananas Baked in Lemon Sauce

Recipe sent by Sheila Fontaine Maidenhead Berkshire

Serves 4–6 people

The advantage of this delightful sweet dish, says Sheila Fontaine, is that it can all be prepared well in advance and just needs popping into the oven 20 minutes before you need it.

1 egg
4 oz (110 g) caster sugar
1½ level teaspoons cornflour (sieved)
Grated zest and juice of 2 lemons
1 tablespoon sherry (optional)
6 medium bananas
1 oz (25 g) butter
Freshly grated nutmeg

Pre-heat oven to gas mark 4, 350°F (180°C).
You will need a 2½ pint (1.5 litre) shallow ovenproof dish.

Begin by whisking the egg and sugar together in a large bowl until the mixture becomes pale and thickened. Then fold in the sieved cornflour, the zest and juice of the lemons and the sherry, folding to mix everything well.

After that peel the bananas and cut them into 1 inch (2.5 cm) thick diagonal slices. Melt the butter in a frying-pan and when it begins to melt and foam add the banana slices. Turn them over gently in the butter and cook them for a few minutes until they begin to change colour.

Then spoon them into the baking dish, cover completely with the lemon sauce and add a generous grating of fresh nutmeg. All this can be done ahead of time. When you are ready to serve, pop them into a pre-heated oven, bake for 20 minutes and serve hot.

Invergarry Whisky and Orange Pancakes

Makes 10 – 12 pancakes

Recipe sent by Lindsay Mackenzie Rogers Invergarry Scotland

It is said that this was Bonnie Prince Charlie's favourite and it is interesting that the great whisky-producing area has a recipe that can hold its own alongside the cognac-laced crêpes Suzette of France. In fact, we think the whisky variety is nicer!

For the pancake batter
4 oz (110 g) plain flour
¼ teaspoon salt
2 eggs
½ pint (275 ml) milk
2 tablespoons oil
A little butter for frying

For the sauce
¼ pint (150 ml) freshly-squeezed orange juice (this is the juice of 3 medium oranges)
Grated zest of 1 large orange
Grated zest and juice of 2 lemons
3 oz (75 g) butter
4 oz (110 g) caster sugar
3 tablespoons whisky

Pre-heat oven to gas mark 3, 325°F (170°C).

To make the pancakes, sift the flour and salt into a large bowl. Then make a well in the centre, break in the eggs, steady the bowl on a damp tea-towel and whisk with one hand (an electric whisk is best). Then gradually pour in the milk with the other hand until you have a smooth, lump-free batter. Halfway through, run a spatula round the edge of the bowl to dislodge any lumps that have clogged there. Lastly add the oil and give another whisk.

To cook the pancakes you need a heavy frying pan, not more than 7 inches (18 cm) in diameter. Get the pan really hot and swirl a knob of butter around to coat the base, and then tip out the excess melted butter on to a saucer, to use when you next need it. Pour 2 tablespoons of batter into the hot pan, swirl it round evenly and as soon as it looks golden on the underneath edge flip it over and brown the other side. Then fold it in half, then in half again and place in a shallow gratin dish. Now repeat until all the pancakes are made; you should get about 12 overlapping each other in rows in the dish.

Now for the sauce – for this you simply melt the butter, stir in the sugar and simmer this for 5 minutes. Then add the orange and lemon juice and zest and bring all this up to simmering point, then add the whisky and simmer for 3 more minutes.

Next pour the sauce over the pancakes – it will look too much at this stage but fear not, the pancakes are going to soak up and absorb the sauce. Now place the dish in the oven for just 10 minutes. If you want to make this in advance you can re-heat it from cold in about 15 minutes, but do not put the sauce over the pancakes until ready to re-heat.

Summer Fruit Brûlé

Serves 6 people

Recipe sent by Virginia White London

This would be a lovely choice for entertaining in the summer when there is a glut of soft fruits – but if some of your glut ends up in the freezer then a taste of summer like this would be a special treat in the winter months.

¼ lb (110 g) blackcurrants
1¼ lb (560 g) soft fruits (including one or more of the following: raspberries, redcurrants, loganberries or blackberries)
4 oz (110 g) caster sugar
8 oz (225 g) whipping cream
8 oz (225 g) plain yoghurt
6 oz (175 g) demerara sugar

You will need a round or oval shallow heatproof dish, approx. 9 inches (23 cm) across by 2 inches (5 cm) deep.

First pick over the fruit and place it in a large saucepan or flameproof casserole. Sprinkle it with caster sugar and then put the pan over a medium heat for about 3 – 5 minutes, only until the sugar melts and the juice begins to run. Now place the fruit in the serving dish and allow it to get quite cold.

After that whip the cream till thick and then fold it into the yoghurt and spread this mixture all over the fruit, taking it right up to the edges of the dish to seal the fruit underneath.

You can then leave it in the refrigerator covered in cling-film. About 2 hours before you want to serve it, spread the surface thickly with the demerara sugar, then pre-heat the grill to its highest setting and, when you are sure it is really hot, flash the dish underneath until all the sugar is brown and bubbling. Now leave it to cool and pop it back in the refrigerator where the sugar will form a crusty surface – wonderful!

Citrus Fruit Brûlé

Serves 4 people

Recipe sent by Helen I'Anson Norwich Norfolk

This recipe received one of the very highest ratings in our FOOD AID test kitchen. It makes a lovely alternative to the summer fruit brûlée in that you can make use of fresh fruit even in the depths of winter.

1 ordinary grapefruit
1 pink grapefruit
2 oranges
3 clementines
¼ pint (150 ml) double cream
¼ pint (150 ml) soured cream
2 oz (50 g) caster sugar
A generous squeeze of lemon juice
3 oz (75 g) muscovado sugar

First, prepare the fruit by peeling the grapefruit then paring the skin from each segment. Peel the oranges, remove all the pith and membrane, then slice them across into rounds about ¼ inch (5 mm) thick. Peel the clementines, then halve the grapefruit segments and orange slices if they are very large but leave the clementine segments whole.

Place all the fruit in a flameproof shallow serving dish (about 1¾ inches or 4.5 cm deep), 2–2½ pint (1.25–1.5 litre) capacity, and spread the fruit out as evenly as possible. Now whip both creams together with the caster sugar and lemon juice and spread this evenly all over the fruit.

Crumble up the muscovado sugar and sprinkle it thickly all over the surface. Pre-heat the grill to full blast for about 5 minutes, then position the dish under the grill, not closer than 2½ inches (6 cm) from the source of heat. This is because this type of sugar burns very readily. As soon as the dish is under the grill, keep turning it, using oven gloves. It will tend to smoke but keep it going until the sugar begins to melt. It will take about 1½ minutes maximum to become hot and bubbling. Do not take your eyes off it for one moment. Then remove it from the grill to cool and chill in the refrigerator till needed.

B. A. Robertson's Coffee Custard Pudding

Serves 6–8 people

Recipe sent by B. A. Robertson

Most people have a love-or-hate attitude to condensed milk: if you're one of the former, then you're bound to have a sweet tooth and this one's for you!

1 × 14 oz (400 g) tin of condensed milk
1 tinful (using the same tin) fresh milk
4 eggs (separated)
10 sponge finger biscuits
8 fl. oz (225 ml) strong black coffee (cooled)
½ pint (275 ml) double cream

To decorate
Toasted flaked almonds
Grated chocolate

Begin by putting the condensed milk, fresh milk and egg yolks in a saucepan, then over a gentle heat stir continually till the mixture thickens to a custard (whatever you do, don't let it boil or it will curdle. If you're short of patience you could cheat by adding a level teaspoon of cornflour mixed with a little cold milk, which will prevent it curdling and enable you to increase the heat slightly. Purists will stir slowly without minding). Pour the custard into a serving dish and leave to cool and set for about an hour.

Next, soak the sponge fingers for a couple of seconds in the black coffee then arrange them on top of the set custard. Whisk the egg whites until they're stiff, then whisk the cream till thickened and fold in the egg whites a little at a time. Spoon this mixture on to the sponge fingers, then decorate with flaked almonds and grated chocolate. Cover and chill in the fridge for several hours before serving.

Note: We like ½ dessertspoon of instant coffee dissolved in 1 dessertspoon of hot water, then stirred into the custard before pouring it into the bowl.

Fudge and Walnut Creams

Serves 4 people

Recipe sent by
Sue Whitehurst
Macclesfield
Cheshire

I am going to introduce this recipe by quoting Sue Whitehurst, who sent it: 'It's so very easy and inexpensive and guests have great fun deciding what the ingredients are. I have never served it to anyone who didn't thoroughly enjoy it and ask for the recipe.'

½ pint (275 ml) whipping cream
½ pint (275 ml) natural yoghurt (not the set variety)
4 heaped tablespoons of soft brown sugar
2 oz (50 g) walnuts (roughly chopped)

All you do is whip the cream until it is nicely thick. Then using a metal spoon, fold in the yoghurt to blend the two evenly. Next, spoon the mixture into 4 wine glasses and sprinkle a heaped tablespoon of brown sugar on to each one.

Pop them into the refrigerator and leave overnight. Next day the sugar will have melted and formed a fudgy layer on the top. Before serving sprinkle each one with chopped nuts.

These quantities can be adapted to any number of people, as long as you use the same proportion of yoghurt to cream.

Orange and Lemon Iced Pudding

Serves 8 people

Recipe sent by
Catriona Thomson
Alloa
Clackmannanshire

This has a lovely fresh tangy flavour which doesn't suffer at all from the effects of sub-zero temperatures. It's made in a loaf shape then sliced for serving but if you wanted you could use an ice-cream scoop and serve it in stemmed glasses.

½ oz (10 g) butter
2 oz (50 g) ginger biscuits (crushed to fine crumbs with a rolling-pin)
3 eggs (size 3)
4 oz (110 g) caster sugar
½ pint (275 ml) double cream
Zest and juice of 1 orange
Zest and juice of 1 lemon
2 oz (50 g) flaked almonds (lightly toasted)

To serve
Fresh orange and lemon slices

You'll also need a 2 pint (1.25 litre) loaf tin.

First of all prepare the tin by buttering the sides and base with the butter. Next, sprinkle the sides and base with the ginger biscuit crumbs to coat it all as evenly as possible.

Now separate the eggs into two roomy mixing bowls. Begin by whisking the whites – preferably with an electric hand whisk – until they reach the soft peak stage, then gradually whisk in the sugar about 1 oz (25 g) at a time until you have a thick meringue mixture.

Next whisk the cream up well with the egg yolks. Then, using a metal spoon, fold the meringue mixture into the egg-and-cream mixture, followed by the orange and lemon juice and grated zest. Lastly fold in the flaked almonds.

Pour this mixture into the loaf tin and put in the freezer until firm – preferably overnight. When you want to serve, remove it from the freezer an hour or so before serving. Turn it out by running the base of the tin under hot water, then ease it out with a palette knife. Decorate with thin slices of orange and lemon cut into halves. Serve cut into slices.

Left to right: Upside-Down Ginger Apple Pudding page 146; Summer Fruit Brûlé page 160; Invergarry Whisky and Orange Pancakes page 159.

Phil Collins' Chocolate Ice-Cream Pie

Serves 8 people

Recipe sent by Jill and Phil Collins

For some years now I have kept constant company (via the stereo in my car) with the tape albums of Phil Collins and Genesis. Because I love their music it's a great thrill to me personally to have a recipe from Phil's beautiful wife.

This recipe can be adapted by using either coffee or chocolate chip ice-cream (or toffee and almond would be rather nice!) with a plain biscuit crust. One thing is certain, it must be good quality ice-cream to start with. If you use vanilla, it's lovely served with a chocolate fudge sauce (see below) poured over just before serving.

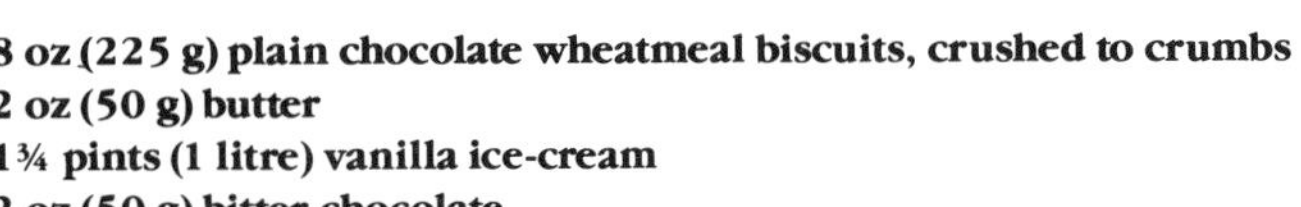

8 oz (225 g) plain chocolate wheatmeal biscuits, crushed to crumbs
2 oz (50 g) butter
1¾ pints (1 litre) vanilla ice-cream
2 oz (50 g) bitter chocolate

Pre-heat the oven to gas mark 5, 375 °F (190 °C).
You'll also need a sloping-sided pie tin or dish 9½ inches or 24 cms diameter (top measurement).

First crush the chocolate biscuits finely and put them into a mixing bowl. Then heat the butter gently in a small saucepan and mix this into the crumbs. Now press the crumbs into the base and sides of the tin, and pop it into the oven to bake for 10 minutes. After that remove it and leave to get completely cold.

Empty the ice-cream into a bowl and quickly whisk it to soften slightly and become spreadable (don't let it melt completely, though). Then spread half the ice-cream in the biscuit-lined tin, and grate half the chocolate over the surface. Now spread the remaining ice-cream over and finish off with the rest of the chocolate on top. Cover the pie with foil or clingfilm and freeze for at least 1½ hours before serving.

Chocolate Fudge Sauce

1 small tin of evaporated milk
4 oz (110 g) bitter chocolate

Break the chocolate up in a small basin and pour in the milk. Now set the basin over a pan of barely simmering water and leave the chocolate to melt until you have a smooth velvety sauce. Allow it to cool and thicken, then serve spooned over portions of the ice-cream pie.

Rhubarb, Orange and Ginger Ice

Recipe sent by
Rita Tyler
Reading
Berkshire

Serves 4 people

This is lovely made in spring with the early rhubarb which has a very fresh, tangy flavour.

1 lb (450 g) rhubarb
6 oz (175 g) sugar
3 eggs
1 teaspoon gelatine
Grated zest and juice of 2 oranges
2 tablespoons ginger wine
4 pieces stem ginger (chopped small)
¼ pint (150 ml) double cream (lightly whipped)

Begin by washing the rhubarb and cutting it into 1 inch (2.5 cm) lengths, then place them in a saucepan with 1 tablespoon of water and stew gently for 5–8 minutes or until the rhubarb is tender. Then purée it with 4 oz (110 g) of the sugar, either in a liquidiser or food processor.

Dissolve the gelatine in a small basin with 1 tablespoon of water, place the basin in a small pan of barely simmering water and leave it to dissolve and become completely clear. Now add the zest and juice of the 2 oranges and the 2 tablespoons of ginger wine to the gelatine.

Next whip the 3 whole eggs with the remaining 2 oz (50 g) of sugar until they become thick and creamy then beat them together with the gelatine mixture. Gradually beat in the rhubarb purée followed by the chopped stem ginger and lastly fold in the lightly whipped cream.

Pour the mixture into a 2 pint (1.25 litre) soufflé dish and freeze. Take the dish out of the freezer and place in the fridge for 2 hours before serving. Serve with either macaroons or sponge fingers.

June Whitfield's Fresh Lemon Cheesecake

Serves 6 people

Recipe sent by
June Whitfield

June says this is a great favourite with her family and much loved by her dinner-party guests. We loved it too.

For the biscuit case
2 oz (50 g) butter
4 oz (110 g) digestive biscuits (crushed to crumbs)
1 oz (25 g) brown sugar

For the filling
12 oz (350 g) cream cheese (softened)
3 oz (75 g) caster sugar
Juice of 2 large or 3 small lemons (you need about 6 tablespoons)
Grated zest of 1 lemon
2 tablespoons cold water
½ oz (10 g) gelatine
¼ pint (150 ml) double cream

You'll need a 7 inch (18 cm) flan tin or dish, 1½ inches (4 cm) deep.

First prepare the biscuit case by melting the butter in a saucepan. Then remove it from the heat and add the crushed biscuits and the brown sugar. Mix these together well then turn the whole lot into the flan tin. Press the mixture firmly around the sides and base, then chill in the refrigerator for half an hour.

Meanwhile put the cheese, sugar, lemon juice and zest in a bowl and beat until smooth (an electric handwhisk will do this in seconds). Now measure the water into a small bowl, sprinkle in the gelatine, stir and leave until it turns spongy. Then stand the bowl in a pan of hot water and stir until the gelatine has dissolved and become transparent.

Next, strain the gelatine into the cheese mixture, stirring it in well. Whip the double cream until it is just stiff, then fold this into the cheese mixture. Now turn the whole lot into the crumb-lined flan tin, and chill in the refrigerator until needed (but for at least 2 hours).

Chestnut Cheesecake

Recipe sent by
Lesley Beever
Ilkley
W Yorkshire

Serves 8 people

In the summer it's so easy to put soft fruits on top of cheesecakes, but in winter it needs something a little different. We feel this is an ingenious idea.

1 × 5.29 oz (150 g) packet Nice biscuits
2½ oz (60 g) butter or hard margarine
½ teaspoon mixed spice
8 oz (225 g) cream cheese
1 oz (25 g) icing sugar (sifted)
2 level teaspoons powdered gelatine
8 oz (225 g) sweetened chestnut purée
2 egg whites
4 fl. oz (110 ml) double cream

You will need an 8 inch (20 cm) loose-based sponge or flan tin, lightly oiled.

First make a crumb crust by finely crushing the biscuits in a food processor or with a rolling pin and a lot of pressure. Gently melt the butter in a saucepan, remove it from the heat and stir in the crushed biscuits and spice. Spoon it into the prepared tin and press it down firmly and evenly. Cover it with clingfilm and chill in a fridge until firm, at least 30 minutes.

Meanwhile, put the gelatine with 2 tablespoons of cold water into a small bowl and stand this in a pan of barely simmering water. Stir it until the gelatine has dissolved, and has become completely clear and transparent.

Then in a large mixing bowl beat the cream cheese till smooth and blend in the icing sugar. Next take 6 oz (175 g) of the chestnut purée (leaving the other 2 oz (50 g) for decoration) and stir this into the cheese mixture. Then stir in the dissolved gelatine and beat it until smooth.

Finally whisk the egg whites till stiff and carefully fold them into the mixture. Pour this into the biscuit base, smooth the top and place in the fridge to chill and become firm, about 3 hours. Before serving remove the cheesecake from the tin. Whisk the double cream and then combine it with the remaining chestnut purée and, using a palette knife, carefully spread it over the surface of the cheesecake.

PRESERVING

Notes on Preserving

Making your own jams and chutneys is easier than you might think if you've never attempted it before. Here are a few notes which I hope will reassure you.

Equipment

There are certain items of equipment which will help to make your preserving easier, but they are not essential.

A heavy gauge aluminium *preserving pan* will last a lifetime and has the advantage of being wide and open at the top (so the vinegar can reduce more effectively). However, a large thick-based saucepan – without the lid of course – can quite safely be used instead.

Likewise *preserving jars*, which seal down with their own lids, are useful but not vital: any sized jar, filled to the top, will do. But a couple of words of warning: vinegar corrodes metal, so make sure your lids are plastic-lined when bottling pickles and chutney. Paper or cellophane covers are fine for jams and marmalade but *not* for pickles: they are not completely airtight and the vinegar will inevitably evaporate during long storage and the chutney will shrink.

Ordinary *gauze* (from the chemist) is perfectly adequate for holding the spices to suspend in the chutney, and *waxed paper discs* for sealing can be bought from most stationers. In an emergency you can cut your own from the waxed paper found in breakfast cereal packets.

Testing

Your chutney is ready when the vinegar has reduced sufficiently. You can test this by running a wooden spoon across the surface of the chutney to make a channel in it: if this channel remains imprinted for a few seconds, without being filled with vinegar, then the chutney is ready.

When testing for a set with jam or marmalade, a cooking thermometer clipped to the side of the pan can be some guide (though I confess the steam doesn't make reading it any easier). Setting point should be reached when the mixture reaches 220°F (104°C). However, there is an alternative, which I invariably use, and that is the cold plate test.

For this you need to have about four small plates ready in the freezing compartment of the fridge. When the fruit has boiled for the stipulated time, take the pan off the heat and place a teaspoonful of the jam on to one of the chilled plates. Let it cool for a few seconds, then push it with your finger: if you can see that a crinkly skin has formed on the surface of the jam, it has set. It not, boil it for a further 5 minutes then repeat the test – and so on until a skin forms.

Bottling and storing
Before you use any jar for preserving it should be washed in warm soapy water (lids as well), then thoroughly rinsed in warm water and well dried with a clean towel. To be on the safe side I personally pop the jars into a moderate oven for 5 minutes, and pour the preserve in while the jars are hot. Chutney can be poured in as soon as it's ready, but leave jams and marmalades for 15 – 30 minutes after setting (so the fruits can settle).

Fill the jars as far up to the neck as possible, then immediately place a waxed disc over the surface. Stick the labels on the jars when cold, otherwise they will very soon peel off. Store in a cool, dry and preferably dark place – and in the case of chutneys leave them for at least 3 months before eating so that they can mature nicely.

Sweet Cucumber Pickle

Makes 4 – 5 lb (1.8 – 2.25 kg)

Recipe sent by
Mrs S Mumford
Plymouth
Devon

If you like this sort of thing make plenty – we devoured half a large jar of this in one sitting when we served it with the *Scandinavian Spiced Herrings* on page 43.

3 large cucumbers
3 large onions
2 oz (50 g) salt
1 pint (570 ml) white wine vinegar
1 lb (450 g) soft brown sugar
½ level teaspoon turmeric
¼ level teaspoon ground cloves
1 tablespoon mustard seed

First of all thinly slice the cucumbers, leaving the skins on, and then thinly slice the onions. Now take a large colander and layer the onions and cucumbers in it, sprinkling each layer with salt. Then place a suitably sized plate over them and press it down with a heavy weight. Place the colander over a dish or bowl to catch the escaping juice and leave it like that for 3 hours. Then pour off or squeeze out as much liquid as possible.

Now put the vinegar, sugar and spices into a large saucepan and stir over a medium heat until the sugar has completely dissolved. Next add the drained cucumbers and onion and bring it up to the boil. Then simmer uncovered for *1 minute only*. Remove the pan from the heat and, using a draining spoon, spoon the cucumber and onion into jars.

Next boil the spiced vinegar mixture uncovered for 15 minutes and then pour it into the jars. Seal the jars and label when cold. Store for a month before serving.

Honeyed Pickled Onions

Makes 10 lb (4.5 kg)

Recipe sent by
Sylvia Lewis
Timperley
Cheshire

Why is it that shop-bought pickled onions are never ever the same as homemade? Although it is tiresome peeling the onions I really believe it's worth it – all you need is a good radio programme whilst you peel them.

For the brining
5 lb (2.25 kg) pickling onions (peeled)
8 oz (225 g) cooking salt
4 pints (2.5 litres) water

For the spiced vinegar
2 pints (1.25 litres) malt vinegar
½ oz (10 g) pickling spice
5 oz (150 g) honey
12 oz (350 g) granulated sugar

Place the onions in a large bowl, sprinkle with the salt and pour over the water. Cover the bowl with a plate to keep the onions submerged, and leave them to soak overnight.

Now, make the spiced vinegar by placing the vinegar,

pickling spice, honey and sugar together in a saucepan. Bring this slowly up to the boil, stirring to dissolve the honey and sugar, and simmer for 5 minutes. Then leave overnight.

Next day strain the onions, dry them a little in a cloth, pack them into cold clean jars, and then strain the vinegar and pour it over the onions. Seal and label the jars and store for 6 weeks before using.

Runner Bean Chutney

Recipe sent by Kathleen Field Bungay Suffolk

Makes 6–7 lb (2.7–3 kg)

'There comes a time in the summer when the family says "oh no, not runner beans again!" Well, they must be picked and this is what to do with them,' says Kathleen Field. Actually, it is so lovely with cold pork or a ploughman's lunch that I recommend you make plenty!

2 lb (900 g) beans (weighed after trimming and slicing)
1½ lb (700 g) onions (chopped)
1½ pints (850 ml) malt vinegar
1 heaped tablespoon cornflour
1 heaped tablespoon dry mustard powder
1 tablespoon turmeric
8 oz (225 g) soft brown sugar
1 lb (450 g) demerara sugar

First of all put the chopped onions into a preserving pan or large casserole or saucepan with ½ pint (275 ml) of the vinegar. Bring them up to simmering point and let them simmer gently for about 20 minutes or until they are soft.

Meanwhile, cook the sliced beans in boiling salted water for 5 minutes, then strain them in a colander and add to the onions. Now in a small basin mix the cornflour, mustard and turmeric with a little of the remaining vinegar – enough to make a smooth paste – then add this paste to the onion mixture. Pour in the rest of the vinegar and simmer everything for 10 minutes. After that stir in both quantities of sugar until they dissolve and continue to simmer for a further 15 minutes.

Then pot the chutney and seal and label as directed on page 173. Keep for at least a month before eating.

Hot and Sweet Chutney

Recipe sent by
Miss J Wheelwright
Leeds

Makes 6–7 lb (2.7–3 kg)

This is good served with curry or spread on cold beef sandwiches and the contributor recommended it with bangers or pork pie – don't worry about the 'hot' being too hot as it does mellow with storing.

1 lb (450 g) apples (weighed after peeling, coring and chopping small)
1 lb (450 g) green or red tomatoes (skinned and chopped small)
8 oz (225 g) figs (chopped)
1½ lb (700 g) dates (chopped)
8 oz (225 g) seedless raisins
4 oz (110 g) onions (finely chopped)
2 pints (1.25 litres) malt vinegar
2 oz (50 g) salt
1½ lb (700 g) dark brown sugar
½ oz (10 g) ground ginger
10 dried chillies (chopped)

All the fruit and the onions can be chopped very successfully in a food processor. Then begin by placing the apples, tomatoes, figs, dates, raisins and onions in a preserving pan with 1 pint (570 ml) of the vinegar. Cover the pan with foil and simmer until the fruit and onions are tender – about 20 minutes.

Then remove the foil and add the rest of the vinegar and the salt, sugar, ginger and dried chillies. Stirring thoroughly, let everything come to a very gentle simmer and let the chutney cook gently for about 3 hours, stirring now and then to prevent it sticking. The chutney should be smooth in texture and all the vinegar absorbed (see note on page 172).

Pour the chutney into hot, clean jars and seal and label when cold.

Pear and Pepper Chutney

Recipe sent by
Mrs M Day
Borehamwood
Hertfordshire

Makes 5 lb (2.25 kg)

We love the subtle flavour of this chutney. It is a wonderful way to use a glut of windfall pears, but even if you don't have that excuse you should try it anyway.

4 lb (1.8 kg) firm pears (weighed after peeling, coring and chopping finely)
1 lb (450 g) onions (finely chopped)
1 lb (450 g) tomatoes (skinned and finely chopped)
2 green peppers (de-seeded and finely chopped)
1 lb (450 g) demerara sugar
8 oz (225 g) seedless raisins
2 cloves garlic (crushed)
A pinch of cayenne pepper
1 teaspoon ground ginger
1½ pints (850 ml) ready spiced pickling vinegar
½ oz (10 g) salt

First place the pears, onions and tomatoes in a preserving pan and cook them over a very gentle heat for about 20 minutes or until the onions are soft. Then add the rest of the ingredients and cook gently for approx. 1½ hours or until the chutney is thick – stirring everything now and then with a wooden spoon to prevent it sticking.

Then pot the chutney in clear warm jars, seal and label when cold and store for 2 months before using.

Autumn Fruit Chutney

Makes approx. 8 lb (3.6 kg)

Recipe sent by Mrs P D Hall Bromley Kent

This is a chutney to make in the late summer or the autumn, when there's a glut of plums, tomatoes and windfall apples.

2 lb (900 g) plums
2 lb (900 g) ripe tomatoes
2 lb (900 g) cooking apples
½ lb (225 g) chopped stoned dates
¾ lb (350 g) onions
1½ pints (850 ml) malt vinegar
¾ lb (350 g) brown sugar
6 oz (175 g) sultanas
1 oz (25 g) salt
1 oz (25 g) mustard seed
1 oz (25 g) celery seeds
½ teaspoon ground cloves
½ teaspoon ground ginger
¼ teaspoon mace

Start off by preparing the fruit: slice and stone the plums straight into a very large saucepan or preserving pan, then skin and slice the tomatoes and add them to the plums. Next quarter, core and peel the apples, chop them quite small and add them to the pan, then finally peel and chop the onions small and pop them in too.

Now pour in the vinegar, and bring it all up to the boil. Simmer (uncovered) until everything is soft and pulpy – this will take about 20 minutes. After that add all the remaining ingredients, stir and boil gently for about 30 minutes, stirring frequently, or until no free liquid remains (see the notes on chutney-making on page 172).

Leave the chutney to cool and settle, then pour it into warm clean jars and label them when cold.

Fresh Apricot Chutney

Makes 4 lb (1.8 kg)

Recipe sent by
Edith England
Nantwich
Cheshire

Edith England, who sent this recipe, says it is lovely served with poultry, especially with duck. She also says that it is *not* really mature until 3 months storing by which time it develops a superb flavour.

3 lb (1.35 kg) fresh apricots (2½ lb or 1.15 kg after splitting and stoning)
1½ lb (700 g) onions
8 oz (225 g) seedless raisins
1 pint (570 ml) malt vinegar
1½ teaspoons salt
1 tablespoon mustard seed
1 level teaspoon chilli powder
½ teaspoon cinnamon
1 level teaspoon turmeric
1 lb (450 g) soft brown sugar
Grated zest and juice of 1 orange and 1 lemon

Finely chop, process or mince the apricots and onions and then place them in a preserving pan or large saucepan with the raisins. Then add half the vinegar, the salt and spices and cook gently, with the pan covered with foil, until the fruit skins and vegetables are completely tender, about 30 minutes.

Then add the remainder of the vinegar, the sugar and the zest and juice of the orange and lemon, bring everything to the boil and continue to simmer very gently, stirring frequently until the vinegar has been evaporated and absorbed and a smooth consistency has been reached. This will take 2 – 2½ hours and it will be a lovely mahogany colour.

Finish by filling warmed, clean glass jars to the brim, and immediately cover with a top which is airtight and vinegar resistant and then add the labels when cold.

Plumberry Jam

Makes 3 – 4 lb (1.35 – 1.8 kg)

Recipe sent by
Mrs E Smith
Banbury
Oxon

This is an ideal preserve for country people who can wander off and gather the real things from the hedgerows in September. Combined with the plums, it will provide a lovely taste of autumn in the winter months.

1½ lb (700 g) Victoria plums
9 oz (250 g) blackberries
2.2 lb (1 kg) granulated sugar
1 tablespoon lemon juice
Knob of butter

First, halve and stone the plums and place them together with the blackberries in a preserving pan or large heavy saucepan and simmer them gently in their own juices for about 15 – 20 minutes or until the fruits are really soft.

Then add the sugar and lemon juice, keeping the heat low, and stir with a wooden spoon until the sugar has completely dissolved and there are no traces of sugar grains still clinging to the spoon when you lift it out. Then add the butter and bring the mixture to a rapid boil and boil for about 12 – 15 minutes or until setting point is reached (see page 172).

Take the pan off the heat and allow the jam to cool slightly for 15 minutes before potting in hot, clean jars and sealing.

Tangerine and Almond Marmalade

Recipe sent by
Miss M Penhale
St Albans
Hertfordshire

Makes approx. 4 lb (1.8 kg)

Tangerines are not easily available nowadays but we made this with something called Mineolas, described as having a different tangerine flavour. We thought it quite delicious!

1 lb (450 g) tangerines
2 large lemons
2 pints (1.25 litres) water
3 lb (1.35 kg) sugar
1 oz (25 g) blanched almonds (cut into slices lengthways)

First scrub all the fruit and then dry it. Cut each one in half and squeeze the juice, reserving it in a bowl. Next thinly slice all the peel into strips. Put the juice, peel and 2 pints (1.25 litres) of water into a large saucepan or a preserving pan. Bring everything to the boil and then simmer very gently without covering until the peel is *absolutely tender* (you should be able to squeeze it apart with your thumb and forefinger); this will take about 30 minutes.

Take the pan off the heat, stir in the sugar and let it dissolve. Then return the pan to the heat and boil until setting point is reached (see note on page 172), ours took 30 minutes to set.

Remove the pan from the heat, let it settle for 15 minutes, and then stir in the almonds. As soon as the marmalade is cool enough and the fruit and nuts have stopped floating on the surface and are distributed evenly throughout the liquid, pour into warmed jars and cover with a waxed disc. Seal and label when cold.

On plate: Plumberry Jam page 179. In dish: Tangerine and Almond Marmalade.

Loganberry, Apple and Mint Preserve

Recipe sent anonymously

Makes 3 – 4 lb (1.35 – 1.8 kg)

This, the sender says, can be used in the same way as cranberry sauce either cold or warmed with sherry to make a sauce for poultry.

1 lb (450 g) loganberries
1 lb (450 g) apples, weighed after peeling, coring and chopping small (early unripe windfalls do well for this)
2 lb (900 g) granulated sugar
Freshly-picked mint leaves, packed to the ½ pint (275 ml) level in a measuring jug (then finely chopped)

First place the loganberries in a large saucepan and warm them gently over a low heat until the juice begins to run. Then add the apples and continue to cook very gently until the apple has cooked to a pulp.

After that add the sugar and stir over a gentle heat until all the sugar has dissolved. Now add the mint and bring everything up to a rapid boil and boil for 5 – 10 minutes. Then allow the preserve to cool and settle for about 30 minutes before stirring to distribute the mint evenly, then pouring into clean, warm jars. Seal down and label when cool.

Wholefood Mincemeat

Recipe sent by David Sulkin

Makes 3 – 4 lb

This is a unique recipe for mincemeat and nothing like anything we've ever seen before. It is also extremely good for the health conscious as it contains no animal fat and no added sugar, and it will keep, so our sender says, for up to a year.

8 oz (225 g) dried bananas
8 oz (225 g) dried apricots
8 oz (225 g) raisins
5 oz (150 g) sultanas
2½ oz (60 g) orange or tangerine peel (fresh)
½ teaspoon mixed spice

¼ teaspoon ground ginger
¼ teaspoon ground cloves
¼ teaspoon freshly grated nutmeg
1 lb (450 g) apples (grated, including peel)
3 tablespoons concentrated apple juice
8 oz (225 g) creamed coconut
4 fl. oz (110 ml) brandy
Juice of 1 lemon

First separate the dried bananas and chop into pieces about ¼ inch (5 mm) thick, then chop the apricots and add those to the bananas, along with the raisins, sultanas and spices.

Now chop the orange peel into small pieces and boil it in 4 fl. oz (110 ml) of water for 5 minutes (this will kill the toxins in the peel and soften it). Then drain it in a sieve and set aside to cool.

Now rinse the apples under a running tap, dry them well, then using a fine grater grate the apples into the bowl containing the dried fruit. As you do this sprinkle a little lemon juice on now and then to stop them going brown. Next grate the creamed coconut into the bowl, then add the cooled peel and the brandy. Stir and mix everything thoroughly. Then pack into jars and store either in the fridge or in a very cool place until needed. Use as conventional mincemeat.

BASIC RECIPES

Chicken Giblet Stock

This stock is useful not only for soups, but also for chicken casseroles, cooking rice and making gravies and sauces.

12 oz (350 g) chicken giblets (washed)
2 pints (1.25 litres) cold water
1 carrot (cut into chunks)
1 onion (quartered)
1 celery stick (halved)
1 leek (sliced)
6 whole black peppercorns
¾ teaspoon salt
A few parsley stalks
2 pinches dried herbs (or sprig of fresh thyme)

The general rule is to use 1 pint (570 ml) water per set of giblets, or if you're buying frozen giblets (which are a godsend for stock) use 6 oz (175 g) giblets per 1 pint water. If you are using fresh giblets and don't need the liver for making a stuffing, do add it to the stock as well – I think it adds real richness of flavour.

Just put everything into a large cooking pot, bring to the boil, skim the surface to remove any scum, then simmer gently with the lid almost on for 2 hours. After that strain the stock, cool it and remove the fat from the surface before using or freezing.

Chicken Carcass Stock

Use the same vegetables, herbs and flavourings as in the above recipe, adding them to the cooking pot along with the broken-up carcass of the bird (plus any odd bits of bone and skin). Add enough cold water to cover, then proceed as above.

Fish Stock

1 lb (450 g) fish trimmings (whatever your fishmonger can rustle up for you)
1 pint (570 ml) water
1 onion (quartered)
2 sticks celery (chopped)

A few parsley sprigs
1 bayleaf
¼ teaspoon dried thyme
¼ pint (150 ml) white wine
Salt and freshly-milled black pepper

Simply place the fish trimmings in a large pan with the water, wine and the rest of the stock ingredients, season with salt and pepper, then bring up to simmering point. Simmer for about 20 minutes (without a lid on), then strain and reserve the stock.

Quick Vegetable Stock

1 stick of celery (cut in half lengthways)
2 medium carrots (split in half lengthways)
1 large onion (sliced)
A few parsley stalks and celery leaves
12 black peppercorns
2 bayleaves
A little salt
1 – 1½ pints (570 ml – 850 ml) cold water

Simply place all the ingredients in a small saucepan, cover with a lid and bring everything up to the boil, then boil briskly for 10 minutes. Then strain (and discard) the vegetables, and the stock is ready to use.

Fresh Tomato Sauce

For 2 people

1 lb (450 g) ripe tomatoes (skinned and chopped)
1 small onion (finely chopped)
1 clove garlic (crushed)
1 teaspoon tomato purée
1 dessertspoon fresh chopped basil (or ½ dessertspoon dried basil)
1 tablespoon olive oil
Salt and freshly-milled black pepper

The best way to skin the tomatoes is to plunge them into boiling water and let them stand in it for a minute or two, then you'll find the skins slip off very easily. Chop up the flesh quite small.

Then heat 1 tablespoon of olive oil in a saucepan and soften the onion and garlic in it for 5 minutes without letting them brown, then add the tomatoes, tomato purée, basil and a seasoning of salt and pepper. Give everything a good stir then cover the pan and simmer gently for 15 minutes. After that take the lid off and simmer for a further 10 – 15 minutes for the sauce to reduce slightly.

Vinaigrette Dressing

1 level teaspoon salt (if possible, rock salt)
1 clove garlic
1 rounded teaspoon mustard powder
1 tablespoon wine vinegar
Freshly-milled black pepper
5 – 6 tablespoons olive oil

Take a pestle and mortar and crush the rock salt to a powder, then add the peeled clove of garlic and pound that with the salt till it turns into a smooth paste. Next add the mustard powder, vinegar and a few twists of freshly-milled pepper and mix these thoroughly into the paste, using a fork. Finally add the olive oil and, just before dressing the salad, pour everything into a screwtop jar and shake vigorously to get everything well and truly blended.

Alternatively (if you don't have a pestle and mortar), add the salt, crushed garlic, mustard, vinegar and pepper straight to the screwtop jar, leave for a few minutes for the salt to dissolve, then add the oil and shake like mad.

Quick Mayonnaise

Makes ¼ pint (150 ml)

This version does not turn out quite so thick and bouncy as the real homemade version, but it is still excellent and better by far than the commercial versions.

1 large egg
¼ pint (150 ml) groundnut oil
½ teaspoon salt
Freshly-milled black pepper
½ teaspoon mustard powder
A drop of wine vinegar

Break the egg straight into the goblet of a blender or food processor, then sprinkle the salt, pepper and mustard on top of it. Have the oil ready in a glass measuring jug, then switch on the machine. Now pour the oil – in a thin and steady trickle – through the hole in the top on to the rotating blades. When all the oil is in and the mixture has thickened a bit, switch off then add just one drop of vinegar and blend this in. Store the mayonnaise in a well sealed screwtop jar in the fridge for up to a fortnight.

Note: For a garlicky mayonnaise you can add 1 crushed clove of garlic to the egg before adding the oil – but only if you intend to use the mayonnaise straightaway (*ie* don't store the mayonnaise with the garlic in it).

Croûtons

For 4 people

2 oz (50 g) bread cut into small cubes
1 tablespoon olive oil

Pre-heat oven to gas mark 4, 350°F (180°C).

Spoon the oil on to a small baking sheet then spread it out evenly with the back of a tablespoon. Arrange the cubes of bread on the sheet, and turn them over in the oil so that they can soak it up and get a good coating.

Bake them in the oven for 10 minutes or until crisp and golden brown. Try not to forget about them – they can get burned quicker than anything I know!

For garlic croûtons Follow the method above, but this time spread a crushed clove of garlic over the baking sheet along with the oil.

For cheese croûtons For these you need to place the oil and the cubes of bread in a small bowl, stir them around to soak up the oil, then sprinkle in 1 dessertspoon of freshly grated Parmesan. Stir the cubes around again to get them coated with the cheese, then arrange them on the baking sheet and bake as above.

Spiced Pilau Rice

Serves 4 people

This fluffy yellow rice, fragrant with spices, is lovely to serve with curries.

Long grain white rice measured up to the ½ pint (275 ml) level in a glass measuring jug
Boiling water measured up to the 1 pint (570 ml) level in a glass measuring jug
2 oz (50 g) butter or 4 tablespoons oil
1 small onion (finely chopped)
1 inch (2.5 cm) whole cinnamon stick
¾ teaspoon cumin seeds (crushed)
2 cardamom pods (crushed)
1 dessertspoon ground turmeric
1 bayleaf
Salt

Melt the butter or oil in a thick-based saucepan and soften the onion in it for about 3 minutes. Then stir in the spices, bayleaf and salt and allow a minute or two while the heat draws out their fragrance. Next stir in the measured rice and when it's well coated with oil and spices, pour in the boiling water. Stir once, put on a tight-fitting lid, and simmer gently for 15 minutes or until the rice is tender. Tip into a serving dish straightaway, fluff with a skewer and remove cinnamon before serving.

Thanks to . . .

Caroline Liddell, Mary Cox and Heather Owen for round-the-clock recipe testing. Valerie Hart for typing the manuscript.

Bifulco butchers for supplying meat for testing.

Bridge Marketing Support Services Ltd for coping with the flood of mail.

Books for Cooks for lending premises.

Anne Charlish, Caroline Elderfield, Caroline Liddell, Susan Platt and Maggie Ramsey for editorial work.

F. N. Colwell for ideas for the FOOD AID logo.

Jean, Penny, Victoria and Jenny at Centre Marketing and Media Services Ltd for organisation of sponsorship.
Assisted by: Clifford Diamond of the Hoskyns Group Ltd; British Rate and Data; The Process Plant Association; Ace Microsystems Ltd; Brother; Newman Books Ltd; The Retail Consortium; The Hotel and Catering Industry Training Board; The Food Manufacturers Federation; The Hotel Catering and Institutional Management Association; Audits of Great Britain Ltd; Beryl Elliot.

Deloitte, Haskins and Sells Media Group for financial, tax and audit advice.

Securicor Ltd; Longstone Ltd; National Carriers Contract Services; Tel-Ser Transport Co. Ltd; Ireland Freight Services; National Carriers Ltd (Parcels Division).

The following manufacturers of this book for giving both their time and financial assistance:
Chorley and Pickersgill Ltd, Leeds, West Yorkshire (typesetting, origination, printing and binding);
Fletcher & Sons Ltd, Norwich, Norfolk (cover origination and printing);
P. Gray Ltd, Croydon, Surrey (paper merchant);
Redwood Burn Ltd, Trowbridge, Wiltshire (printing and binding);
Townsend Hook Ltd, Snodland, Kent (paper manufacturer).
W. Photoprint, Focus Typesetting Ltd and TWP Services Ltd for their help with publicity material.

Lacquer Chest, Tables Laid, Scene Two, Table Props and Linen Hire for lending props for photography free of charge.
Graham Gardner and Magnum for free studio transport during food photography.

The illustrations were generously donated by the following artists: page 8 Glyn Boyd Harte; page 22 Brian Grimwood; page 34 Debbie Cook; page 58 David Sim; page 78 Christopher Brown; page 90 Lynda Gray; page 110 Nicola Gresswell; page 126 George Hardie; page 144 Alan Adler; page 170 Chloe Cheese; page 184 Linda Smith.

Photography: Grant Symon. Stylist: Penny Markham.
Food preparation for photography: Berit Vinegrad.
Painted backdrops: Andy Knight.
Film for photography donated by Keith Johnson Photographic Ltd and processed by Carlton Fox Ltd.
Retouching by Steve Bloom.

Book design: Linda Blakemore and Glyn Davies.

Portraits on the following pages were kindly supplied by Hodder and Stoughton page 24; Donald Innes Studio page 92; London Features International Ltd page 166; Ken Lo page 39; Network/Steve Benbow page 115; Rex Features pages 10, 106, 162; Snowdon page 54; Woman's Own/Brian Moody page 28; Woman's Own/Victor Watts pages 41, 128; April Young Ltd page 168. Portraits on pages 37, 62, 99 and 132 are BBC copyright.